# Island Fever

By

Janis R. Scott

ISBN: 1-4107-2093-4 (E-book)
ISBN: 1-4107-2094-2 (Paperback)

Library of Congress Control Number: 2003090961

This book is printed on acid free paper.

Printed in the United States of America
Bloomington, IN

Cover Art by Sonja Ashmore McGriff

1stBooks – rev. 07/03/03

Dedicated to a fellow "Arkie", Billy Bob Thornton, whom <u>I do not know</u>; but wish I did.

Also to my <u>family</u> – Veto McGriff, Lee, Joyce, Leanne, Sonja, Myles, Mark, Earlene, and Earl Gene and <u>friends</u> – Nancy Nako, Irv, Caprice, Ursula, June, Norma, Betsy, Terri, Joanie, Susie, Donna, Doyle, "Mexico Joe", Chuck Porter and Charles S., and x's Robert Dennis Burns, David D., Ali M. and Durrett C. McGriff, the eye of the hurricane – all have contributed in some way toward me being the person I am.

Janie pulled her wallet from her overstuffed purse; she screamed another 'shut up back there!' to the screeching kids in the back of the van and paid two dollars toll for the trip over the causeway to the island.

"How much for the U-Haul behind?" she asked the lady in the tollbooth.

It suddenly occurred to her how often they'd need to leave the island and come back onto it in the normal course of living. "Do island residents have to pay this toll?" she asked and sighed when she heard the 'yes' as a response.

"Damn!" she said and smiled back at the tanned face of the attendant.

She handed Janie a receipt. "Maybe you can take this off your taxes," she soothed.

Janie put the car into gear and began the drive over the long causeway toward the beautiful island beyond.

The bay stretched along both sides of the narrow causeway. The bridge humped upward toward the incredibly blue sky.

The shadow of 'their' island smudged the distance. The children screeched louder.

This was a far cry from the corn and wheat fields of Iowa. None of the four children had been on an island. None of them had seen the ocean-or as in this case-the gulf.

Janie and Jake Meleski had attended a farm convention in Miami six months before. While they were in Miami they decided to rent a car and return to Iowa the long way. They had flown to Miami and missed the scenery along the way. They had loved the beautiful coastline around Miami and they felt they were long overdue an actual vacation. They'd had a few short trips and some camping outlets with the children to state parks in Iowa and a few neighboring states.

Even the outings had grown less frequent as farmers more and more felt economic pressure.

It had been these economic pressures that had prompted Jake to research and write for farm aid programs and had given them the opportunity to attend the convention in Miami, Florida.

Jake's literature, among sheaves of others, was being presented and distributed. His 'common sense' approach had earned much acclaim. They'd used it themselves almost as an instinct for survival. They had prospered or hung on when all around them many friends, members of the community, and other family members of neighboring farms had gone broke.

They'd watched neighboring farm equipment sold at auction and houses sold or abandoned as the farmers had loaded their remaining possessions and moved on.

Middle aged and old farmers alike had been forced to seek new careers in new places. Families and friends were torn apart and uprooted.

Jake had been determined to keep the farm he'd inherited from his parents and the adjoining one Janie and her twin sister Janna had inherited from their parents.

She only had one sister and Jake was an only child, which she was sure had promoted the large family they had and were adding to. There were four screeching children in the back of the van and she was six months pregnant with twins.

She looked down at her bulging midriff and smiled. They were returning to the island where she was sure she'd become pregnant. She had even dreamed of the twins the day after she'd seen the house. The dream had been strange. The twins were girls and she had been one of them. The dream often rose to haunt her. When she found herself pregnant with twins she, somehow, wasn't surprised. She even knew their names for she had dreamed that, also. They were Janna and Janis. She and her twin sister were Janie and Janna.

As Janie drove across the causeway she felt a sense of homecoming. Jake followed in the U-Haul. It had been a long trip from Iowa but they had stopped often and allowed the children to sightsee and play at a number of tourist attractions.

She and Jake had decided the twins would be the last children they'd have. Jake was getting a vasectomy after they were safely born.

She smiled back at her children through the rear view mirror. First they'd had Alicia, then they'd wanted a little boy and Jake, Jr. came along, then they'd wanted a sister for Alicia and she nagged for one repeatedly. Felicia was born. Next they decided Jake Jr. needed a brother so as though to order little Jeremy joined the family. Janie smiled as she thought, "And then we ran out of excuses and here I am again!" She was already regretting the time had come when they'd have to quit and she'd not have a small baby or toddler to cuddle.

The trip along the coast had resulted in a family-owned home on the island.

Jake's uncle and aunt and their children would spend their share of time there this year. Then Janie's cousin and her family would have a turn and Janie's Aunt Tesse's son Wilbur and his family would have a turn.

Janie and Jake were setting up the household and having the first turn. The rest had drawn numbers from Jake's old felt hat.

The U-Haul that Jake was driving held collective castoffs. "You will bring it all together somehow," Janie was assured.

"'Eclectic' I think it's called," her cousin said.

"Fancy for 'junk'", Jake's uncle laughed.

Loading up the U-Haul had been fun. The furniture, linens, dishes and bedding, and other items, had come from the various households and attics.

Everyone had met at Janie and Jake's house for an early morning breakfast and then the loading had begun amid comments and laughter as each item was unloaded from pickup trucks and onto the U-Haul.

Ideas for a sort of slap dash decorating scheme had woven through Janie's thoughts as she'd driven across the states from Iowa southeast toward the island.

Many of the items she was transporting had been handmade a century or so ago. There was a handmade trestle table with benches to match, a couple of bureaus with a dozen or so small drawers, three large handmade clothes closets-one of walnut, another of golden oak and the other of a satin smooth hard maple. Three ornate iron bedsteads had chipped paint showing a palette of various colors under their topcoats. Another donation had been the big brass bed that had been in Janie's family for as long as anyone could remember. It was in need of an extensive polishing. Janie sighed at the thought. "Maybe I can get the kids to do it," she decided. The big fluffy feather bed that went along with the bed was rejected—"Lord! We'll never need that!"

Janie had laughed remembering the warm soft breezes and the pleasant nights with the soft air from the gulf.

"We won't even need clothes—just jeans, shorts, a few cotton shirts, and maybe two dress up outfits—just in case," she'd laughed. "We are going total native!"

Jake and Janie had found the place by accident when they'd made a wrong turn.

They had been coming from Miami in the car they'd rented to drive back to Iowa and sightsee along the way. When they got lost they decided to just explore along the small road they found themselves on as they'd taken the left fork instead of the right one they should have taken.

The road had narrowed and then was intersected by a road that showed a long curved bridge to the left.

"Which way?" Jake had asked.

Janie could see the sparkling water of the bay and what appeared to be a smudge of an island in the distance.

"Let's explore a little longer and then we can ask directions," she'd said. "Let's go over that bridge!"

Jake had smiled at her childlike enthusiasm. "You're the navigator!" he'd said.

"Oh! Yeah! I'm the navigator now that we're lost!" Janie laughed.

Jake had grinned at her with a twinkle in his gorgeous eyes. "See how smart you are?" he'd teased. "And expensive"—he added at the toll bridge proclaiming a two dollar fee for crossing to the island.

They asked directions at the tollbooth and found they had driven only a few miles off their originally planned route.

"Could we see the island anyway?" Janie had asked. The desire to see the island was strong. She felt like she HAD to see it.

The sun was setting as they drove over the bridge. A rainbow of colors spread as far as the eye could see on the rippling water and the sky above.

Janie gasped in delight. "I've never in my lifetime seen anything so beautiful!"

Janie had been enthralled by the scenery that was so different from Iowa as they had taken the small road toward the intersection. The narrow road had been overhung with large twisted trees slung thick with mats of greenish gray Spanish moss waving from their weathered-looking limbs.

Scrub palmetto and skinny pines rose out of a jungle of vines and undergrowth that pushed the road from each side. The shiny leaves and buds of magnolia trees growing wild in the tangled vegetation was like a scene from a gothic setting in a movie.

The emergence from the jungle-like scene to the strip of sandy beach along the bay was sudden. The waves and colored waters stretched all the way across the water until the distant barrier of the smudgy island interrupted it.

The causeway ran between the sunset waters. "It's like riding through a rainbow!" Janie said softly.

Jake reached over and squeezed her hand.

The causeway approached the tall humped bridge. As they drove over it, it seemed to reach the colorful sky above. The wavy rainbow of waters danced far below. "It's so high!" Janie said.

"Boats pass under the bridge, I suppose," Jake said.

The island became more visible as they descended the humped bridge and entered the long curvy sweep of the causeway. The island appeared to float on the ripples of the bay.

Before they reached the island the marsh grasses came into view. The grass appeared to be black.

"Look!" Janie pointed, "That grass is BLACK!"

"Probably dark, dark, green," Jake guessed.

"Looks like ugly black grass," Janie said. "I'll bet there are alligators and snakes hiding under it!" Janie shuddered.

Janie looked away from the grass to a small marina curving into the shore on the other side. A tiny sailboat bobbed beside a little pier. A couple of small wooden boats were close by.

They drove between the marsh and the marina. As they drove onto the island they could see the waters of the gulf a few blocks in front of them.

"Narrow, isn't it?" Jake remarked.

They saw a couple of small stores with gas pumps, a couple of bar and grill establishments, a restaurant, a bank and some real restate offices, and a large inn of some sort. Further down on the other side of the island on the gulf a motel could be seen on the right stretching along the gulf.

Jake and Janie drove to a parking place in front of tiny dunes and a shell-strewn beach.

"Let's pull off our shoes and walk on the beach!" Janie said, her eyes were shining with happiness.

Jake caught her hand as she stepped out of the car. They walked between the small dunes onto the beach. The gulf held so many colors of blue and green—even some purple Janie noticed.

"How different this is from the rainbow bay with the sunset on it!" Janie laughed, as she dodged a wave and picked up some tiny shells it left as it receded back toward the next oncoming wave.

"I wish the kids could be here," she said and could see them in her mind's eye-gathering up seashells and frolicking in the waves.

Jake and Janie walked along the shore with the waves dancing on and off their feet. As darkness began to eat the colors of the waters they turned back to leave.

As Jake backed the car into the street, Janie asked, "Jake, Honey, could we please stay here tonight?"

"Are you tired, Sweetheart?" he asked.

"No, I'm just so happy here I don't want to leave," she answered.

"There's a motel over there," Jake pointed to the motel that sprawled along the beach.

"Did you notice that pretty white two story hotel with the porches all around as we came on to the island?" she asked.

"Over there?" Jake pointed to the looming structure a block or so away on the main drive onto the island.

"That's it," Janie said.

"Suits me," Jake said and drove the small distance to park beside the picturesque two story white frame structure with blue shutters and a porch surrounding the upstairs. Rocking chairs scattered around the porch looked inviting in a homey sort of way.

As they walked up to the porch in front a stained glass door panel threw pretty colors out from the light inside.

As they entered a tinkle of glassware came from behind French doors.

They peeked in to see a man placing silverware on snowy napkins. He looked up as they entered, as though surprised to see guests.

"Are you here for dinner?" he asked.

"We'd like to check in first," Jake said, adding politely, "if there's room."

Janie felt a giggle in her throat and held it back. There had been no other cars in the parking lot.

"I'll ring for Miss Lela," the man said, ushering them back into the hallway.

A small desk stood beside the stairway. The man pushed a button and a chime sounded somewhere else.

Tapping heels ushered in a tall thin lady. Her blue eyes smiled. "Guests!" she exclaimed.

The business of checking in was simple. She suggested they take a room with a view of the gulf. "The view is so pretty in the morning," she said.

The room was lovely—all white wicker and rose patterned polished cotton drapes, pillows and bedspread. A couple of pastel-colored seascapes hung on the wall.

"I think I'm on the honeymoon I dreamed of when I was growing up," Janie said, almost shyly.

"Better late than never," Jake said and leaned to kiss the tip of her nose. Their eyes met and held—the sweetness of their love mirrored there.

They stood on the balcony and looked out at the last of the fading light upon the water. A faint roar of the waves seemed exotic to Janie's ears. Everything was so different from Iowa. The heat was cooling down and a soft breeze brought strange and unique scents of the island's essence to her nostrils. "It even SMELLS exotic here!" she breathed deeply.

They bathed and dressed and went downstairs for a delicious seafood dinner.

After dinner they strolled over to a couple of bar and grills and had a beer at each place. "The natives are sure friendly," Janie laughed. A number of people had spoken to them, some even asking where they were from. None of the people seemed to have ever been to Iowa.

A band began to play and a few people danced. Jake stood up and held out his hand to Janie. "Want to dance?" he asked.

Janie was surprised. "We haven't danced in years!" she laughed, "and even then it was seldom!"

"Well, after all, it's our honeymoon," Jake said, drawing her into his arms.

They danced a couple of dances and Janie whispered, "Want to go to our room now?"

Several people called out goodbye as they left.

They walked back to the inn holding hands.

Jake and Janie stood on the porch for awhile before going to bed. He held her close by his side with his arm around her shoulders. She leaned her head against his shoulder and closed her eyes. She felt such peace and happiness. The soft breeze, the elusive smells, and the almost humming roar of the surf were like an aphrodisiac. She turned to Jake and pulled his face down to hers. The kiss became ecstasy and she was surprised to feel herself lifted up into Jake's strong arms and carried back into their room. "I've carried you over the threshold," he whispered, his voice hoarse with desire.

He slowly let her down to stand before him. He reached to pull her cotton tee shirt from the waist of her shorts. He ran his hand over the curve of her full breast and reached behind her to unfasten her bra.

Janie closed her eyes as she felt him slide down the zipper on her pants and begin to draw them over her hips. It had been so long since they'd taken time to fully explore each other. Sex had become almost habit when they had time to actually have it.

Janie felt her breath come faster as Jake knelt to slide her shorts down and then reach for the sheer white panties she'd worn under them. His face was close and she could feel his warm breath through the thin fabric. His hand traced its way down her leg as he drew the panties downward. He lifted each foot gently and removed the shorts and panties from around her feet. She heard the soft sound of them being tossed aside. His face touched her stomach and moved downward. His breath felt hot and his tongue tickled her into shivers of anticipation. She felt herself arch forward and little ripples began to pulsate between her legs. He teased her until she was weak. Finally she could stand it no longer. She raised herself on tiptoe and cupped his head with both hands drawing him into the soft quivering place between her legs. His tongue was hot and active and she moaned with desire. She suddenly shoved him away—"Wait!" She took his arms and tried to draw him up but suddenly sank to her knees to face him. She reached out and tore his tee shirt over his head. His hands fought with his zipper. Suddenly he stood drawing off his shorts and underwear in one quick movement. He stood naked before her. His manhood was stiff; the veins were bulging with desire. She leaned to take him into her mouth slowly. She heard him moan and he pulled her away. "Bed!" he gasped and gathered her up in his arms. She sank into the soft bed and felt him above her. Her hand guided him into her soft pulsating body and as hard as they tried to wait they couldn't hold back. Jake took her fast and hard when he realized it couldn't last. They climaxed together both crying out in release. They didn't have to worry if the children would hear—and it was better than the honeymoon had been for she'd been a virgin and it had taken awhile for her to have sex without a bit of pain. After a few days, though, the sex between them had been great. She remembered her first climax. It had taken her by surprise. She had cried from joy. Jake had teased her.

Jake pulled her to him and they cuddled close. The soft roar of the gulf came into the silence of the room. The movement of the big plantation fan above them was just visible in the twilight of the room. The light from the porch barely touched the darkness turning their bodies into planes of shadow and light.

Peace and happiness filled Janie's heart. Soon she heard Jake's soft breathing and the little snores that accompanied his early stages of sleep. She smiled and snuggled closer and fell asleep.

*

The brightness of the morning sun came through the window and lay itself across Janie's face. She screwed up her eyes and reached blindly behind herself to find Jake.

The bed was empty. "Jake!" she called softly, then again louder. There was no response.

The bathroom door was closed and she tapped on it before opening the door. It was empty.

Janie hastily bathed and dressed. She thought of the wonderful 'honeymoon' night they had enjoyed together.

Janie wandered out to the porch and looked around.

The gulf sparkled into miles of jewel-like dancing lights. Froth sprayed upon the tips of waves. The blue and aqua waters spread toward the dark green horizon and met with the contrast of a soft blue sky.

A breeze tickled through the tall golden strands of sea oats that cropped out through the small sand dunes. A few people walked along the white sand beach, often bending to pick up or examine some small thing along the way—seashells, Janie supposed. A few children played at the waters edge and Janie thought of their children at home in Iowa. She wished they could see the gulf. They had never been very far from Iowa. She knew how delighted they'd be.

Janie wondered if Jake had taken a walk along the beach. She wanted to go out and frolic along the waves. She was so happy—so full of energy and the sheer joy to be alive.

Janie went back inside and pulled on her socks and Reeboks. While she was tying her shoes Jake came in juggling a small newspaper, a handful of literature, a sack and large cup of Jr. Food Mart coffee.

"The natives are still friendly," he smiled.

"And how about you?" Janie smiled impishly.

"Very friendly!" Jake laughed and came over to kiss her. "Thank you for last night," he said and pulled her close.

13

"Want a re-run?" she asked.

"Maybe before we check out, huh?" he said and ran his hand over her breast sending a thrill down her body. He opened the small sack and took out doughnuts and napkins. He had stacked two cups together and he poured them both some still hot coffee.

"They only serve dinner here at the inn," he said.

They sat outside on the rocking chairs and sipped their coffee and nibbled the doughnuts.

"So the natives are friendly—no big pots or kettles boiling out there amongst the palmettos," Janie smiled.

"Only for boiling shrimp, I think," Jake said reaching over to grab her last piece of doughnut.

"You rat!" Janie laughed and swatted him. She picked up the pamphlets and leafed through them.

"It's so beautiful and peaceful here," Janie said as she looked at the quaint houses on stilts for sale. Some of the houses were on one level but most were on pilings—some of them small and others quite large. Some of them had large French doors and verandas running along the front and sides. Many of them were constructed from natural wood. "A lot of cypress and cedar," Jake said.

"Could you imagine one of these in Iowa?" Janie asked.

"It would be colder than a welldigger's butt in Idaho!" Jake said. "The cold air would assault the house all around—here it keeps the house cooler and also keeps it above possible high waters."

"I'd love to just look at some of these houses," Janie said. "They are so curious looking."

14

"We could, I guess," Jake said.

"NOW?," Janie asked.

"Sure," Jake said and she pointed to a real estate office across the way. "Let's try that one." Jake hugged her.

"Let's go then," he said, "we're burning daylight."

Janie knew they'd have to leave the island soon. She felt reluctant to go.

*

The realtor was a perky little redhead who still seemed to be enthusiastic about taking them around even after they explained they were just wanting to look out of curiosity.

The girl's name was Debbie. She asked questions about where they were from, how far away Iowa was and if they were on vacation.

Janie saw Jake blush when she said, "We're on our second honeymoon."

Debbie led them to her four-wheel drive Wagoneer and after they were on their way to what became a sightseeing tour she gave them some island and local history.

Debbie pointed out the nest of an osprey, which was a bird that had become practically extinct. The nest was high up in a tall slender tree. A wooden platform had been erected under the nest and wire surrounded the base of the tree. The wire was to keep raccoons away from the nest as well as other predators.

Everything was bathed in sunlight. The houses that were pointed out to them seemed to be open and airy with a great deal of natural woods used in building them. They were mostly weathered into soft shades of browns, tans, and grays. The open floor plans of the ones

15

they went inside brought perfect blending of the outside elements with the interior, creating an infinite sense of space even in the smaller homes. One home in particular beckoned to Janie.

As soon as Janie saw the house tucked into the palms, palmettos and vine-encrusted surroundings she stared at it as though in surprise. She gasped and goose bumps ran down her arms making her shiver.

"I've seen that house before!" she said to herself even though she knew it was impossible.

"This is the oldest house on the island," Debbie was saying. "It has a great history and some myth attached to it." She was about to drive past the house.

"Could we see it?" Janie asked, her heart beat faster as she waited for the answer.

Debbie had passed the house by then. She stopped and backed up to the overgrown drive. "It's for sale—again," she said.

Jake looked at Janie. "We'll have to get going soon," he said as Debbie walked around the car to join them.

"Just this last one," Janie said. She moved eagerly toward the house.

Thick cedar steps led up to a wide shaded veranda. The two-story house had been built of stone and natural timbers. The long driveway crunched with oyster shells that were packed deep to hold back the voracious vegetation.

Tall pines, twisted and weathered, grew in no particular pattern about the grounds. Scrub oaks and thick vines crowded the base of the trees. Palms and palmettos filled in spaces among the oaks and pines. The little oak trees looked dwarfed and stunted but they were beautiful there under the tortured and twisted branches of the old evergreens. A few glossy-leafed magnolias towered above the stunted oaks. Their leaves were thick and looked waxy in the sunlight. Creamy white blossoms sat among the leaves as big as dinner plates. Yellow jessamine gave off a delicate aroma, and as they approached the porch the heavy scent of gardenia mingled with the breeze.

"That smells like heaven!" Janie said.

"There are several large gardenia trees planted around the grounds," Debbie said. "They are very old."

The smell of the gardenias increased Janie's feeling of déjà vu. A sweet sad feeling overcame her—like a longing for something she couldn't name. She touched Jake's arm as she stepped onto the porch.

Heavy cedar beams supporting the ceiling of the porch spoke of age.

Debbie fitted the key into the lock and creaked open the heavy timbered door. The creaking noise caused Janie to shiver—and somewhere in the shadows of her mind the creak caused a rush of something almost like fear.

Janie looked above the door as though she knew the fanlight would be there.

Debbie held the door open and Jake gently nudged Janie forward. She had stood transfixed upon the threshold blocking entrance to Jake and Debbie. Jake's hand propelled her forward a few steps.

Debbie was chatting with Jake as they moved toward the interior of the house.

Janie was spellbound. A tear formed and slid down her cheek and the word 'home' pushed poignantly at her heart.

Leaving Debbie and Jake, Janie walked upstairs. Her hand trailed the smooth worn wood of the stair's railing. She paused as her fingers touched an indentation in the wood. Leaning forward she read the barely legible words that someone long ago had carved into the wood half way up the stairs. *"David and Janis Forever,"* she whispered aloud. She had known it was there. Her fingers had sought it out like a blind person searching out braille.

"David and Janis Forever," she whispered again as she continued upward.

The room was waiting. It had waited for so long.

Janie traveled the length of the hallway, past several doors without noticing their presence. The room beckoned and she came to it on feet that seemed to walk themselves.

A touch swung the door inward and beams of light threw ray upon ray of brilliance through the window. The shadowy hallway hadn't accustomed Janie's eyes for the sudden surge of light.

Fantasy figures seemed to spring apart—they were etched in silvery light. Dust motes danced in their wake and Janie stared, her eyes trying to pierce the brilliance and know the haunting of some lost memory. A hand touched her shoulder and she screamed.

Jake's voice pulled her back to the world she knew.

"I'm sorry, honey!" he said, touching her hand in apology.

Janie laughed nervously and Debbie giggled.

The view from outside the window became clear. "You startled me," she said as she walked to look out the window.

The bay lay shining and wrinkled with tiny waves beyond a fringe of the dark green grasses that looked black. Twisted pines, palmettos and scuppernong vines entwined in a writhing mixture of trees and vine. Squabby palms clustered together here and there as though to protect each other.

Janie's eyes sought a small hill to the right of the bayside jungle. It was covered with the thick vines and palmettos with twisted oaks running down its sides. Large gray pieces of stone were entrapped in the vines. Hundreds of tiny blue butterflies hovered over the hill flying into a tapestry of color and action.

"They are so beautiful!" Janie exclaimed.

Debbie and Jake looked over her shoulder. "They migrate here every year," Debbie explained.

They turned to leave and Janie turned back a moment to look at the hill out back. The beautiful butterflies seemed so right there. She was pleased to see them.

Janie pressed her hand on the indentations as she walked back down the stairway. Soft echoes whispered almost audibly in the shadows of the upstairs hallway.

Janie felt reluctant to leave the house. She looked back almost hungrily. It seemed so right to be there and also so strange.

Janie still looked backward over her shoulder as Debbie pulled out of the driveway and drove past the house.

"You seemed to love that house," Debbie said.

"I do," Janie said.

"It was bought and sold often over the years. The present owners have had it for a good many years and have had it for sale since shortly after they bought it. They've lowered the asking price for half of what they originally wanted."

Debbie paused for awhile and added, "Some people aren't affected by the house as you were, but everyone who looks at it seems to have some sort of reaction."

"Do you think it's haunted?" Janie asked, feeling foolish as soon as the words were out of her mouth.

Debbie looked uncomfortable. "I don't think I personally believe in ghosts," she said and changed the subject.

Jake and Debbie spoke of real estate and the building going on the island.

Janie thought of the house—mostly she thought of how strangely familiar it seemed both inside and out.

Debbie was telling Jake how very inexpensive the house was compared to the other property being offered for sale on the island. The property was just over an acre with the house sitting in the middle of the acre.

Janie listened in silence.

*

Later that afternoon, Janie and Jake sat beside the shore. Small waves lapped their toes; larger ones threw surges of water against their chests often toppling them backward onto the sand.

Janie was deep in thought as she let the warm waves toy with her feet. She felt so relaxed—so at peace. Jake had his arm around her shoulders and they laughed together when the larger waves came to buffet them around. She licked salt spray from her lips and glanced at Jake.

"You're quiet; are you tired?" Jake asked. He had been watching her for some time as she gazed abstractly across the undulating body of water.

"I want the house," Janie heard herself blurt out the impossible desire.

"Janie?" Jake asked, smiling with a look of surprise on his face. "Has the sun addled your brain? Do you have island fever, honey?" He reached over playfully and felt her forehead.

"No, listen," Janie said, her eyes serious— "listen to this. Just suppose we bought the house as a family time-share. I heard Debbie and you talking about time-shares on those condos she's handling." Janie trailed off, her eyes pleading with him.

Jake was still trying to deal with the fact that his sane and very practical wife was actually serious. "Now if this were Janna, her sister," he thought, "something like this would be expected—but Janie—NEVER!"

Jake looked at her for a moment, waiting to see if she were in fact joking. She wasn't. He took her hand, "Honey, we just bought those new combines for the farm. How could we jeopardize ourselves by buying property so far from Iowa? We've neither of us been to Florida before now. What makes you think we'd be likely to ever come this way again?"

Janie's chin raised. Jake knew the sign. "I'm damned if she isn't serious!" he thought again.

"It's a good investment at the price it's being offered at," Janie insisted.

Jake was shocked at her persistence.

"But in FLORIDA, Janie," Jake protested. "NONE of us ever got this far away before!"

"If I got three other family members to purchase with us, would you do it then?" Janie pleaded.

Jake saw a sheen of tears film in her eyes. He felt safe in agreeing. "Under those conditions, we could," he agreed, feeling relief at getting off the hook.

Janie flung herself at him and they rolled into the water, waves tossed them around as she hugged him gleefully.

"You're addled for sure," Jake laughed and ducked her. "The sun has fried your gourd and given you island fever!"

"You'll see!" she promised, a wide grin spread across her face. "You'll see!"

*

The early morning sightseeing around the island with Debbie had taken several hours. They had gone from there to the largest of the bar and grills and eaten a really good lunch.

The natives were still friendly. One of the people who had talked to them the night before was there at the bar talking to a couple of other men. Everyone seemed to know each other. Their new acquaintance of the night before sent them over a couple of beers—he had remembered they had Miller Lites the night before. Jake and Janie returned the favor and soon found themselves engaged in conversation with several of the natives. It was much later when they left the bar and grill.

Janie sighed as they got in the car. "I'm so sleepy—what I'd really like is a nice afternoon siesta."

Jake looked at his watch. "Lord! Look at the time! We've lost a good part of the day already." He grinned at her and asked, "What do you think about extending our honeymoon one more night?"

Janie was delighted.

They checked into the inn across the boulevard and got their same room back.

They stripped off their clothes, laughing as they stepped into the shower together.

"How long as it been since we bathed together?" Jake asked.

"Too long," Janie answered as she began to lather him playfully. "It's been years since we've really had time to play with each other. The farm and the kids fill up our lives."

Jake held her close and rubbed the soap between their bodies.

Janie giggled as his erection rose like a barrier between them. Her hands came down to caress it, sliding the soapsuds up and down it's length. Her other hand pulled his head toward her and she tasted soapy water as their lips met. They didn't wait for the bed. Jake took her hand away and rinsed the soap away. His hand went between her legs and he lifted her up. His big strong hands cupped her hips and her legs encircled his waist. The shower wall supported them as he slid her to and fro—at first slowly and then frantically as they fed their appetites for each other.

Janie felt weak as she finished her shower. Jake soaped her hair with shampoo and helped her rinse it. The seawater had made it stiff and unmanageable.

They took turns toweling each other off. Their kisses were tender and familiar.

Janie turned back the cool white sheet on the bed while Jake threw their clothes they'd worn to the bar and grill in the plastic bag the inn had provided. They'd changed their wet clothes at the gas station/convenience store before they went to the bar and grill for they'd assumed they'd be on their way off the island after they'd eaten. Janie's hair had dried but stuck out in all directions. They'd laughed as Jake found a rubber band to pull it back. "Am I presentable now?" Janie had asked. Jake looked around at people in cutoffs and tank tops, shorts and bikini tops, and all manners of dress and undress. "I think you blend well," he laughed.

The hot sun, food, beer, and lovemaking had Janie half asleep by the time Jake slid into the bed beside her. She wiggled her naked butt into the curve of his body. Jake pulled her close with his hairy arm and they slept.

Janie awoke to the sound of Jake moving quietly around the room. She rolled over and smiled as she watched him laying out clothing. He bent over the suitcase and she watched his naked behind open to disclose his manhood swinging between his legs.

Jake spun around when she giggled. "Oh! So you're admiring my behind?" he laughed.

"And your front, too!" Janie said.

"Better watch out!" he warned.

Janie slid from the bed and hugged him close. "I'm so happy," she said, and kissed him.

"Are you hungry or do you want to fool around?" Jake asked.

"What time is it anyway?" Janie asked noticing for the first time that the room was shadowy.

"It's eight thirty and I thought we might go out for dinner and maybe even do a little more dancing before our honeymoon ends," Jake said.

"Then it's a date!" Janie laughed.

They dressed in their jeans and tee shirts. Janie pulled on her Reeboks and Jake dug out a pair of scuffed loafers. They were soon dressed.

The heat of the sun had disappeared and a soft warm breeze was like a caress as they walked hand in hand toward the restaurant aptly named 'Paradise'.

After a wonderful seafood dinner at the 'Paradise' they walked to the bar and grill where they'd been the night before. The band was just starting up when they got there. Several people said 'Hello'. Jake ordered beers and they found a table close to the dance floor.

The bar was busy. There seemed to be a mixture of locals and tourists. It was the beginning of the weekend and the place was crowded.

Jake left coming back with cold Miller Lites. As Janie looked over the crowd she said, "Look, Jake! There's Debbie!"

Debbie sat at a table across the room. Several other people were with her.

"I want to talk to her for a moment," Janie said.

"Now, Janie, you don't have any idea whether you'll be able to sell anyone in Iowa on the idea of time-shares in Florida—in fact I very much doubt you will," Jake cautioned her.

"Maybe not," Janie said, "but I still want a few words with her about the house."

Jake saw the stubborn little lift of her chin. "Oh, Lord!" he groaned to himself.

"She may not be wanting to talk business. She seems to be having a good time there with her friends," Jake cautioned.

"I'll only keep her for a minute," Janie said rising.

Jake watched her walk across the room to Debbie's table. Debbie stood up when Janie approached her table. Jake watched her smile as she spoke with Janie and then introduced her around the table. He saw Janie shake her head when she was offered a chair. She and Debbie spoke for a moment and Debbie came back across the room with her. Jake rose to say hello.

"This probably isn't the right time to discuss this with you," Jake said.

"I know you're leaving early in the morning—so when else?" Debbie laughed taking the chair across from Jake. "In fact, I thought you were leaving today until Janie just told me you'd postponed it until in the morning. I'm really very happy to see both of you again!"

Janie said, "You were right, Debbie. I'm really drawn to that house. Jake and I couldn't afford it alone but I heard you talking to him about time-shares and I think there is a possibility I can get some of our relatives involved and we can buy it that way."

Jake listened in silence. He felt Janie was doomed to disappointment and felt sad and still shocked at her tenacity.

"Do you think the house will still be on the market for a while?" Janie asked.

"There's no guarantee," Debbie said. She seemed to think for awhile before speaking. "I'll be frank with you, Janie, at the risk of perhaps disillusioning you about the house. No one seems to be able to live in that house for very long. It may be that they hear gossip and then let their imaginations take hold, but so many of the people say the place is haunted. I've been there several times and I, personally, haven't seen or heard anything. People on this island have very little to do and gossip abounds. Everyone here knows each other except the tourists. When the tourists buy and become residents then they seem to get connected with the grapevine. So, what I'm saying, in my experience, is that if the house does sell—just wait and it is possible it will be vacant again. The only thing is that any new owner might up the sale price which is low now." Debbie paused and looked at Jake and Janie.

Jake expected the news of the house's history to be a deterrent to Janie's enthusiasm. He was amazed to see Janie's eyes light up. "I think it's enchanting!"

Jake's throat was dry. He took a sip of his beer. "Ah, Debbie," he began. He hated to acknowledge he could even believe in a ghost. Their existence seemed so far fetched to him, yet he had to ask, "Have the—er—ghosts ever hurt anyone? Do they throw things around, or what?"

"Not really," Debbie said. "Some of the people say they saw—or almost saw—something from the corner of their eyes. Some people think they hear voices. It's been no more than that but still the people leave."

Janie sat silent. She knew she'd have the house, someday at least. Suddenly she couldn't wait to get back to Iowa and try to get the family involved in a time-share.

After Debbie returned to her friends Janie and Jake ordered another beer. The music was loud and several couples were dancing. Jake and Janie danced several dances before they went back to the inn.

Janie laid out their clothes for the early morning trip back to Iowa. As she slid into her modest nightgown she smiled, thinking of the way they'd fallen asleep naked after their shower that afternoon. They didn't dare go naked in Iowa with the kids likely to pop into their room at any given time.

Jake came to stand behind her and his arms held her close as she was turning back the sheets on the bed. She stood snuggling herself into his tall, lean frame. He nuzzled her hair and whispered, "How is the honeymoon going?"

Janie turned in his arms and pulled his lips down to hers. A breathless moment later, she asked, "Does that answer your question?"

Jake turned out the lights and they slid between the cool crisp sheets together. He held her in his arms and slowly began to caress her body. Their lovemaking was long and tender; neither of them wanted it to end.

Satiated with each other, drained of passion and filled with a deep and tender love, they fell asleep and Janie dreamed of the twins.

\*

Jake woke Janie up early the next morning. "Up, sleepyhead," he coaxed.

Janie had slept deep and sound and her dreams had been ones of joy. She stretched and opened still half-asleep eyes.

"What time is it?" she asked and closed her eyes again.

Jake sat beside her and gathered her close. "It's time to hit the road, that's what time it is," he laughed and tickled her.

"Okay, you win, I give up!" Janie gasped. "Just stop—don't tickle!" she giggled.

"I'll get coffee while you shower and dress," Jake said.

Janie stretched out in the bed after he left and thought of the dreams. Her hand caressed her stomach. "Janis and Janna," she whispered, "are you there?"

She had just showered and dressed when Jake came in with doughnuts and coffee. They sat on the rocking chairs on the porch and watched the sun break the horizon as it peeped a red eye out from behind the gulf throwing pink and rose lights into the scuttling night clouds. The gulf roared softly and the exotic smell of the island mingled in the breeze.

"Could we just walk on the beach one more time? I want to gather seashells for the kids," Janie asked.

"We'll have to do it soon," Jake said, "for we need to drive a full day today."

"I want to go home and I miss the kids," Janie said, "but I hate to leave. Isn't that strange?"

"Yes, it is," Jake agreed. "I think you like this honeymooning," he teased.

The sun was low and round on the horizon and the clouds were stained with soft pinks and blues when Janie and Jake reached the beach. They had brought along a couple of plastic grocery bags for the seashells.

When they had picked up enough shells to satisfy Janie they turned to walk back to the car. Jake hugged Janie close. "This is a beautiful place," Jake said. They stood for awhile and watched the soft swell of the gulf as it rolled endlessly toward the horizon.

Janie touched her stomach, "Jake, I'm pregnant," she heard herself say.

"Honey! Why didn't you tell me! Do you think it was a good idea for you to travel this distance in your condition?" Jake answered in concern. "Do you remember how careful you had to be during a couple of your pregnancies?"

Janie smiled. "You may think I'm nuts but I know I got pregnant last night. I dreamed of them, Jake. We are going to have twin girls. I even dreamed their names: Janis and Janna. The dream was so real and the babies were so sweet and when I woke up this morning I knew it was true. We're going to have twin girls—Janis and Janna."

Jake looked horrified. "Janie, are you sure you're okay? You know ever since we've been on this island you've been so unpredictable; you've not been yourself. It's been wonderful as you know—it's been heaven—our honeymoon we never had. But Janie, you have surprised me in so many ways."

"I've never felt better, or been any happier, Jake," Janie said. "It's strange to me, too. I'm positive there's nothing wrong with me and I do believe I'm pregnant. The dream was too real."

"I think I'd better get you back to Iowa before I lose you altogether," Jake smiled but a worried look hovered in his eyes.

Janie gave one last look at the gulf. She was sure she'd be returning. She felt such a part of the island: the roar of the gulf, the pelicans that flew in formation over the water hunting for fish. Their dives into the water head first at break neck speed for their catch. A school of porpoise rolled and frolicked just off the shore, little birds ran swiftly over the sand on skinny legs, and seagulls floated everywhere. All of this seemed a part of Janie and she wanted her children to know it, as she seemed to. "Yes", she admitted to herself, it was odd, all of it, yet she felt so happy and so at peace.

*

30

How Janie did it Jake never comprehended but she did persuade the others to invest in the property.

She had armed herself with sheaves of literature on the island, the area, and real estate on the island. She had taken picture after picture of the house, the beach, birds, vegetation, sunsets, sunrises, and her sales pitch must have been that of a professional for she got the house.

When Janie had all the agreements and financial details of the time-share worked out, she called Debbie. She was so happy.

Debbie had sold the house that week. Janie sobbed as though her heart were broken. "Honey, she told you it might sell," Jake said, patting her as she clung to him in despair.

Everyone was disappointed for Janie had them all pumped up. Janie began having morning sickness and at Jake's insistence bought a home pregnancy test. She was pregnant. She cried frequently and Jake became concerned. He forced her to go to see a doctor. Her depression was diagnosed as a product of her pregnancy and the doctor wanted to give her medication for the depression. Janie refused. She tried to force herself to be cheerful but Jake saw the shadows in her eyes.

Three weeks after the house sold, Debbie called. Janie answered the phone.

"Your house is up for sale, again," Debbie said. Janie let out a squeal of delight.

"So we can have it?" Janie asked.

"I'm going to have to be honest with you," Debbie said. "You may not still want it after I've told you what happened."

"Is the price a lot higher? Is that it?" Janie asked.

"No," Debbie answered, "the price is the same and the new owners want to sell it as soon as possible for they had invested all their money in the house."

"That's GREAT!" Janie said, she was so happy, so excited.

Jake had heard the phone ring and Janie's squeal of delight. He stood watching her happiness at the phone call. She hadn't been happy since she'd lost the house.

"There are things I have to tell you, Janie, before I can in good conscious sell you that house," Debbie said.

"Okay," Janie said and waited.

"This is difficult," Debbie said, "for I still don't believe in ghosts."

Janie smiled. She had been afraid the termites were eating the house up or something structurally was wrong.

Debbie cleared her throat before speaking, "Well, according to the people who bought the house their first night there was one of sheer hell. There were sounds of glass breaking and when they looked around nothing was broken. There were screams and angry voices and someone sobbed all night long. The children swore someone came into their rooms. There were sounds of footsteps running down the stairs and the front door screeched as though it were being opened. They searched the house and nothing was wrong. They stayed a week and each night, and some days, the sounds and sightings continued. During a night of extreme screams, glass breaking, and pounding footsteps, shouts and wild sobbing, the family ran from the house in the middle of the night and wouldn't even return to pack their things. They had movers come in to move them back to Tallahassee. They are threatening to sue for their money back," Debbie said, "so I think I'd better warn you that you might not be comfortable in that house. Of course, if I sell the house to you we can give the people their money back, but then you, too, might have the same problems."

Janie said, "Thank you for telling me, Debbie. We still want the house. What do I need to send you to get this started?'

"One thing you'll have to do," Debbie laughed, "is to send me an affidavit that I've told you the circumstances of the last sale and that you will take the responsibility for anything that may occur as a result of living on that property and in that house. I'll also need some cash for earnest money. I'll send your offer in to the present owners and I'm sure they'll grab the chance to get their money back. I'll send you the paperwork."

"Do you believe that family?" Janie asked.

"It sure seems odd," Debbie said. "I went out there yesterday with one of the other realtors and she and I saw and heard nothing unusual. The house seemed peaceful and calm."

Janie and Debbie supplied each other with fax numbers and Janie assured the doubtful Debbie one final time that they did still want the house.

"What was THAT all about?" Jake asked.

"Oh, the new owners heard about the house being haunted, I guess, and their imaginations got to them. They want to sell the house," Janie smiled.

Jake looked worried. "Do you think it IS haunted?" he asked.

"I thought you didn't believe in ghosts!" Janie teased him.

"Well, I really DON'T," Jake admitted. "Do they want more money?"

"No, the money's the same," Janie answered.

Once again Janie sold the idea of the time-share to the relatives.  She made no mention of ghosts, and now they were on the way to the island to establish the household and have their vacation.  The other owners would follow as scheduled.

Jake following in the U-Haul still had a sense of perplexity over the turn of events. His tongue and cheek agreement to buy the property as a time-share had backfired.  He'd had no idea Janie could persuade family members to contribute in property in Florida. Jake smiled as he thought of Janie's complete turn around from being depressed to being absolutely glowing.  He had been more amazed though to find out they were having twins.

Janie and the kids were already spilling out of the station wagon when Jake drove up in the U-Haul.

Janie stood looking at the house.  The jungle of vegetation around the property seemed sunken in shadow while the house was bathed in sunlight.  It was highlighted with the sunlight.

The kids dashed up the steps onto the porch. Jake reached in his pocket for the keys that Debbie had sent.  He came to stand beside Janie and took her hand.  He dropped the keys into her palm.  "Well you did it, Sweetheart," he smiled.

Janie's hand clutched the keys.  She felt her fingers tremble.  "Home," her heart said again.  "Home".  She opened the door; the creak had always been there, she knew, as the door screeched open.  It had creaked the night someone fled into the night and never returned.  "WHO?" her mind fumbled, and then she wondered, "Am I nuts? I can't possibly remember what I don't know!"

The children stampeded past. Bags and bundles followed as rooms were chosen overhead. "This room's mine!" she heard several voices yell out. No fights ensued so she assumed they'd settled on different rooms.

She waited for the traffic of youthful feet to dash back downstairs then walked upstairs alone. Her fingers traveled the banister and her footsteps lingered halfway up. She felt the depression and her breath caught. "'Forever'," she whispered and walked on.

The room was empty of baggage. "So this is our room," she mused. A dusky light hung in the room. The dust motes were barely visible in their disturbed swirling. A current of cool air brushed Janie's shoulder like a caress as it slid by. The babies in her body seemed to wiggle at the touch.

Janie walked to gaze through the window. The butterflies were gone from the small hill. The sun threw a shaft of light onto a gray stone and Janie turned away to seek the familiar company of her husband and children.

The children were eager to see the beach before darkness set in. Their bathing suits were easily found as they had decided to have them 'ready' when they'd packed in Iowa. "The gulf" had been a big topic of conversation along the way. "The island" was also a source of great interest to them. The children were frantic to get into the waters of the gulf.

A trail led from the house southward over piles of oyster shells, tangles of low vegetation, grasses and clumps of the sea oats that waved from the sandy dunes.

As they approached the shell-strewn sandy beach the children screamed with joy at the sight of the playful dashing waves and little scampering birds.

The house was at the tip of the Island, but not so close as to enjoy the merging of the gulf and waters of the bay that occurred several hundred yards further down the island. The path to the gulf from the bayside home was probably a couple of blocks, Janie figured.

The children ran for the beach. The undulating waters of the gulf that seemed to meet the horizon and merge with the sky thrilled them into shrill exclamations.

Seagulls took flight as the little farmers tried to catch them and the tiny birds with fast thin legs ran frantically before they took wing to evacuate the area.

Four eager bodies flung themselves into the waves.

"It's salty!"  "It burns my eyes!"  "It knocked me down!"  "Here comes a big one!" was screamed in unison.

The children loved it.  Janie and Jake held hands, shouted out cautions, and kept a head count.  They knew the children's excitement.

Jake touched Janie's stomach.  "The next ones will grow up knowing the gulf," he said.

"It's time," Janie answered.

The sun dipped low and spread the gulf with pastel colors and everyone marveled.

The children were difficult to coerce from the water.

Back at the house nothing was in order. Sleeping bags and some mattresses would be used that night.  The household goods and furniture would be unloaded the following day. Jake would ask around to see if anyone were available to help unload the U-Haul.

After the activity at the beach the children were tired. The trip had been long and strenuous for Janie.

She fixed a hasty meal of tuna sandwiches, a fruit salad, and iced tea while Jake helped the children with baths and nightclothes. The excitement and activity kept Janie from feeling the house.

After the children settled in Jake and Janie took tall cool drinks onto the sun porch that ran across the back of the house.

Janie spread a beach towel over the seat of an ancient wooden swing that hung from two rusty chains. "I hope this doesn't break," Janie laughed as it creaked when they moved to and fro. "This is the only piece of furniture in the house!"

They swung gingerly and soon became confident that the rusty old chains would hold. "I'll find a place to buy new chain tomorrow," Jake said. "You know how the kids are; they will be giving this a workout!"

The bay outside the window glimmered in the moonlight and twisted vegetation presented a shadowy framework to enhance the effect of isolation. Now Janie felt the house. Intangible emotions pulled at her heart and mind. The lure was like a drug as she sought more and more of the strangeness she had experienced since she'd first seen the house. She'd turned to speak to Jake about the house but words failed her and logic defeated explanation. "No one could understand," Janie thought and then she said to herself, "except Janna, maybe. This is more like something that Janna, the imaginative one, the writer, would have happen anyway, for after all, aren't I the practical one?" Her lips curved in a smile as her mind left the house to dwell upon her twin sister. "Wild, crazy, impulsive, adventuress. Those were words other people used to describe Janna—but never Janie, for perhaps she alone in all the world understood what made Janna run. Between she and Janna was a bond of unbroken love and a sharing of souls. A merging of selves transversed their unparalleled worlds in which they lived. One of her twins would bear Janna's name and the other would bear the name on the banister, for those were the names that she'd dreamed, and she knew they were the appointed names for her babies. They were named in her dream.

Janie and Jake slept in the room overlooking the bay. They spread their sleeping bags on the hard plank floor. "We'll probably survive," Janie said as she and Jake rolled around trying to find the soft spots where none existed. They both were exhausted and soon slept.

Janie's bed became the big brass bed still on the U-Haul. It was large and soft and mosquito netting swathed the entire bed.

Moonlight filtered through the netting as though it were a soft white fog. Janie reached out in search of her twin. Her groping hand met with failure and she moaned in her sleep. "Janis?" she whispered into the stillness of the room. "Janis?" No one answered. Janie awoke to a flood of tears. "I don't know, Papa! I don't know!" she had cried out.

Janie awoke to find Jake bending over in the moonlight. "Honey," he whispered, drawing gentle fingers across her tear-soaked face. "Honey, it's only a dream."

Janie struggled to cast aside her dream; it held her between her world and something else.

She reached for Jake and pulled him close. "It was so real," she said.

"They are when you first wake up, but I'll bet you won't remember enough of it to tell it to me in the morning," Jake consoled her.

"Maybe not," Janie murmured. She soon fell into a dreamless sleep. Jake's arms held her close.

The next morning she still remembered the dream.

She remembered the lovely room she'd seen through the moonlight and netting and she remembered Papa's angry face. "Who's Papa?" she wondered.

*

The next day was filled with unloading the U-Haul and arranging the truckload of household goods.

Janie placed her sewing machine on the back porch. She planned to shop for fabric and make her own curtains. As isolated as they were they would use mostly sheers except for the kid's bedrooms and the bath. "Simple and airy," Janie thought.

The children howled at the prospect of more sandwiches for they'd made sandwiches from Iowa to Florida. They cheered up when they were promised dinner out. "Seafood," they all decided.

Jake was fortunate enough to get a couple of men to help with the unloading. They were natives of the island and had overheard him asking for help at the island's favorite watering hole.

Janie was already unpacking some of the kitchenware that had been purposefully placed at the rear of the van. She was busy stacking plates on a shelf when she glanced up to see a tall wiry man walk through the house carrying a carton up the stairs. She gasped, her hand flew to her chest and she reached back for a chair that wasn't there. A feeling of happiness flooded her senses. There was something so RIGHT about him walking up those stairs—about him moving in. "MOVING IN? GOD!" Janie shook her head in disbelief. "Where did those stupid thoughts come from?" she wondered. Could it be something to do with her pregnancy with the twins that sent her on those flights of fantasy that kept occurring— that she actually seemed to seek? She laughed at herself. "The PRACTICAL one," she said aloud and smiled at the description. The feeling of happiness remained.

She looked up to see Jake watching her. "You seem happy," he said. "Sure this isn't too much for you?"

"NO, I'm fine. In fact, I couldn't be better," she answered.

"Well, Honey, don't overdo it," Jake cautioned. "The trip alone was more than I felt comfortable for you to undertake."

"I know," Janie said. "You stopped so often along the way I thought we'd never get here! Of course, we all had a lot of fun along the way because of it."

"You'll have to direct us on the furniture— what goes where," Jake said, "but I don't want you to lift anything yourself."

"Who is that man who's helping you?" Janie asked.

"There are two of them," Jake answered. "Locals."

*

David sat sipping a beer. He and his friend were discussing a building project they'd just completed for a 'tourist'. The man had been a bastard to work for and they were more than happy to have completed the job. The man had ultimately been satisfied. But by the time they finished they didn't give a flying frig either way. They just wanted to collect their pay for the grueling, thankless days spent in the blazing sun admist nagging little bouts of ass chewing. The man had learned his boundary before the job was over, for David had twice gathered up his men and tools and left the man standing there steaming and helpless to get the job completed on time without them. Each time the man had to come to him begging to have them come back. The ass chewing had eased off but the man's face had turned permanently sour.

The check was in the bank, the workers paid off and David was beginning to mellow out. They'd stopped at his friend's house, smoked a joint and gone to the bar to have a few beers. A couple of beers down the road, he idly listened to a pleasant-looking man with a mid-western twang to his voice asking for someone to help unload a U-Haul.

Unlike himself, for he was fed up with tourists and island transplants, he asked his partner, "Want to give this asshole a hand?"

His friend shrugged and David said, "We could help after awhile."

The man was grateful. After a round of beers they all left. The guy didn't seem such a bad sort, David decided.

David knew his friend had rather not leave but he came along anyway. Hoyt's girlfriend, Joan, worked at the bar and grill where most of the natives and a good portion of the tourists hung out. She was a tall, blue eyed blonde with 'marital problems'. One of the problems was Hoyt. They were 'in love'. Hoyt was as serious as a dog in heat. Joan was pulled like a tide at full moon—her husband was going to change—hell, he was even going to get a job and go to work! Hope swayed her toward the promise of the big 'change'. Hoyt always worked. He was an oysterman, dark as an Indian, tall, lean, with the oysterman's big hands and large bare feet. His facial bones spoke of Indian heritage. You could easily picture him in breechcloth and tomahawk treading silently through the swamps, as had his Seminole ancestors before.

Creek and Seminole history was richly strewn throughout the area. Arrow heads, artifacts, and pottery shards were found all along the shores of the island where there had once been mounds and Indian encampments.

The man, so far removed from the pampered baby-faced boy she'd found herself married to, fascinated Joan. A boy who took her small paychecks as his due was the complete opposite of Hoyt, who wanted to buy her the things she did without. Hoyt and Joan's liaison was a spreading secret, destined to filter off the island and onto the mainland and bring about possible violent repercussions.

People didn't mess with Hoyt. His friends watched, waited, and some worried. David was concerned. He and Hoyt were close. "We go back a long way," they'd say.

David may have agreed to help unload the U-Haul due to a long time fascination with the old Diehl place. Legend had it that a family name of his had been Diehl and that somehow the Dutch merchant who'd built the home in the seventeenth century had been a relative.

The limited family history that had filtered down to David had led him to believe that he was of French, Dutch and Creek Indian heritage. The Dutch seemed to have been dominant. His fluff of hair was sandy brown with reddish tints, freckles splattered him like a speckled pup and where his cut off jeans covered his lithe hips his skin shone pearly white.

Beyond his elderly aunt and uncle, his past was just that. Typhoid fever had killed both of them when David was just a young teen. He had continued to live in the rickety little house on the edge of the swamp. Things hadn't changed much after their deaths other than his loneliness for them.

He'd worked since he was twelve. The cooking hadn't been hard to do for he ate very little. He'd grown up boiling shrimp outside in the big pot, steaming scallops and oysters by wrapping them in seaweed and burying them under hot coals in a rock lined sandpit. He could catch, clean, and have a fish smoking on an improvised spit in the bat of an eye. He'd watched Aunt Marie make pan cornbread enough times to be able to figure it out. He loved planting and tried to maintain the small garden his Uncle Tiger had grown year after year. David had helped with the garden since he'd been a tiny tot.

David had been three years old when his parent's small dinghy had been sunk in a sudden squall while they fished.

They'd left him with Aunt Marie and Uncle Tiger the night before and he'd stayed on.

As he grew older and able bodied, his youth had been an asset to the aging foster parents.

David roved the rivers and swamps like the untamed creatures he met there.

At ten years old David had come home with a rattlesnake he'd killed miles away. It was huge and had been heavy.

Marie had deep-fried the flesh to a crisp brown crust surrounding the white tasty meat underneath. He'd been so proud.

Tiger skinned the snake and sold the hide with hides he'd collected himself. David's snakeskin was one of the largest ones he sold.

From the age of fourteen David began hiring out as a guide to tourists. When he was older he had an opportunity to study for a charter Captain's license.

He took a job at the marina and took tourists out on fishing excursions.

David had learned to read very young. He hungered for knowledge. The tourists often discarded books in the community dump and he sought them out. He gathered himself a library of extensive information. He loved the crossword puzzle books and grew proficient in solving them.

Between charter fishing he worked at various construction sites about the island.

An elderly woman once told him a story when he was young about a baby who had been abandoned on the doorstep of an Indian family. They had raised the child as their own. Tiger's great grandmother had taken in this child. There were other stories from the old ones that David wished he could remember. Some of the stories were very strange and he was so small when he heard them. He sometimes thought he could almost remember, but the curtain of memory never parted enough for him to glimpse the mystery of those old tales that haunted him with their elusive hints of memory.

David loved the island. He was as much a part of it as the jungle growth, the gulf, sand, and wildlife. He was saddened to see every available inch of the island being bought by outsiders. New houses sprang up like mushrooms.

The new houses were a good source of income though, and David managed to save enough money to attend a vocational school and learn some drafting. He learned to draw blueprints and to figure jobs.

He bought a big flat bed truck, tools and hired on a few workers and began competitive bidding on jobs both on the island and on the mainland. People knew David and loved him. They trusted him.

Women jacked David around somewhat but he met most of them in bars. As he got older they seemed to get younger. They got stuck on eighteen to twenty while he moved on up to his mid-forties.

David drank a lot of beer, had a lot of friends, worked hard, but something always felt like it was missing. Sometimes he'd just jump on his Harley Davidson and ride the cobwebs out of his mind. After the rides he always felt better—for awhile.

*

When David drove up to the Diehl house he experienced the feelings he always felt when he was near the house, feelings he couldn't even describe to himself. The feelings varied. They ran the gamut, scale up and scale down, but always there was the sudden rash of goose bumps on his forearms.

It had first happened when he was a boy messing around the closed house. He hadn't thought of the goose bumps until his arms began to prickle. David laughed, "I forgot but my arms remembered!"

Jake was opening the U-Haul and pulling the boxes toward the doorway. He pointed toward a stack of cardboard boxes and said, "Those go upstairs. Put them in the first room to your left." He gave Hoyt boxes to go to the dining room and he took a large box labeled 'bath'.

David carried the large carton upstairs. He'd never been inside the house. A strange feeling of knowing the house came over him. He had a lifelong fascination with the house. He almost envied the people moving in. Of course he didn't think they'd stay long. No one did.

As David entered the house he saw a lady in the kitchen. She was pregnant and even though she was one of 'the tourists' she seemed so right there in the kitchen.

David thought of the house as he unloaded the household goods. He admired the old handmade furniture, some of it painted long ago, the colors soft and muted. He longed to see the place after everything was put into place. The large armoires were so right for the house. He helped Hoyt carry the heavy headboard of a four poster brass bed upstairs and into a room at the back of the house. The sight of the bed had somehow disturbed him. The room disturbed him even more. He was overwhelmed with a feeling of sadness when he stepped into the doorway. He wanted to cry and was embarrassed to feel tears actually well in his eyes and run down his cheeks. He set the headboard down and walked to look out the window overlooking the bay. His eyes were drawn to the hill covered with heavy vines and a shudder ran over his body as he looked at

the gray stone ensnarled in the vines. Images
that made no sense boiled into a turmoil in
his brain. The pain he felt was real. He
tore himself away from the window and left the
room hurriedly. "No wonder no one stays
here," he thought. The house still drew David
though, for as he left, on impulse he turned
to Jake saying, "If you need any work done on
plumbing, construction, or anything, you could
leave us a message at the Watering Hole where
we met. The people who own it are friends and
I use it as my 'office'."

Jake thanked both men after paying them.
The tall thin, barefoot men had been very
nice. Jake thought he'd have Janie cut off a
pair of his old jeans. He laughed at the
thought of his white legs—legs that saw very
little sun in Iowa where he worked in overalls
even in the summer and had very little leisure
time otherwise. "You've got to start
somewhere," he thought. "I don't guess they
were BORN with those tans!"

*

Between the beach with the kids, short
excursions and fishing off the bay, the house
took Janie a week to finish to her
satisfaction.

The fabric for the curtains had been
purchased and sewn. The gulf breeze fluttered
them throughout the house, except for the
bedroom Janie and Jake shared. "Aren't you
going to put curtains on our window?" Jake
asked when she'd hung the rest and finally
closed up the sewing machine's lid.

"No one can see us; we're at the back of the
house and the view's enchanting," Janie said.

She had planned to curtain the window, had even bought the soft gauzy fabric, cheese cloth like a mosquito net. She'd bought extra thinking to do a whimsical net over the tall brass posts of the bed. As she held the fabric to the window, a feeling of suffocation came so strong that her hand had clutched her throat. The claustrophobia grew as she once again held the fabric over the window. Janie knew she wouldn't be able to shut off the view of the outside tangle of vegetation, the glimmering bay with tiny boats heaped with brown lumps of barnacle-covered oysters, of the sunrise and sunsets over the waters of the bay and of the small hill with the strange gray stones ensnarled with vines.

Finally she had folded the fabric and put it to rest in the lovely old chest she'd placed at the foot of their bed.

The room reached toward the outside, pulling as much of it in as possible.

*

The children loved the island. Each day they discovered new wonders.

The second week was half over and at the end of the third week they'd be packing the station wagon to leave. It would be a couple of months before the next family members would be coming for their brief stay on the island.

Janie had expected to miss Iowa more than she did.

Janie was contended, the children were happy and Jake was running around in cut offs trying to get a tan. He wore his loafers after trying to go barefoot and getting goats head stickers in his feet. "How do they do it?" he'd laughed.

It was in this atmosphere that Felicia had screamed out in fear during the night.

Janie and Jake were instantly out of bed. Alicia was beside her younger sister and the boys dashed in from their rooms. Felicia was crying and her babbling through the sobs made no sense.

Jake scooped her up in his arms. He patted her tangle of curls and shushed her gently.

Everyone waited in silence until she quieted down.

"Now, honey, what was it? A bad nightmare, a scary dream?" Jake questioned.

Felicia snuffled and hiccuped. "I saw her in my room," she said. "She wasn't scary—I was scared."

"Saw who?" Jake asked, still hugging her close and patting her head.

"The lady that Jakie saw one morning—the one who floated down the stairs," Felicia said.

Jake turned to Jakie, "What's this all about, son?" he asked.

"I really saw her," Jakie said.

"Just like you saw the green gorilla in the woodshed and terrified the girls so much they wouldn't go get firewood for weeks?" Jake smiled. "Jakie, son, you've got a great imagination—but don't use it to scare the girls. Sometimes your practical jokes go overboard. Remember our last talk? You scared your mother half to death when you put that rubber snake under the covers in our bed."

"That's why I couldn't tell you," Jakie explained. "You wouldn't believe me."

"Oh, Jakie, got to bed, we'll talk tomorrow," Janie said as she remembered the 'dream' she'd had and not been able to talk

49

about either. "Now scoot, everyone! Get to bed!"

"Felicia, Alicia will sleep with you. It was only a dream, honey." Jake put Felicia back on the bed. Alicia cuddled her sister. Everyone went to bed. The house grew quiet.

Jake and Janie lay close and Jake fell asleep almost instantly.

*

The next day Janie drew Jakie aside, "Tell me the truth and I'll believe you," Janie coaxed.

Jakie's chin rose with that determined look he'd inherited from her. "I DID see her," he said, his face stubborn as he waited for opposition. He seemed very surprised as his mother said quietly, "Tell me about it."

"Well, I woke up thirsty and started downstairs for a glass of water. The bathroom light was on and I didn't turn on a light. I was trying to be quiet because everyone was asleep. I saw her about halfway down the stairs. At first I thought she was running, but then I saw that she was floating—fast—toward the front door. At first I thought it was you—just for a second—then I was afraid. She just disappeared. I went back to bed and the next day I told the other kids and they made fun of me," Jakie waited as though expecting Janie to do the same.

She patted him on the head, "Okay, Jakie, maybe you did see her. What was she like?" she heard herself ask.

Jakie looked pleased. "She was so SUDDEN and FAST—but she was something like you I thought—different—but something like you.

"I think she was crying," Jakie added.

"Enough before you start to embroider!" Janie held up her hands. "Now scat!" she said in the familiar way she had to disperse kids.

Jakie grabbed a cookie and darted off. Someone HAD believed him!

Janie gathered up clothing. Beach towels and sandy clothing was an everyday occurrence.

The bare wooden floors accumulated sand and Janie found herself bribing the children to vacuum every chance she got. The house was perfect with one exception.

Janie decided to ask Jake if they could get a stacked washer and dryer installed. The trips to the laundromat were expensive and time consuming. She'd get the rest of the group to chip in on the cost. "Heck, I got them to buy this place, didn't I?" she giggled to herself.

Janie knew Jake would grumble a couple of minutes but he'd do it. "I love him so much!" she thought.

Jake thought himself to be a gruff bear. She and the kids knew he was a pussycat when it came to them. Jake had been her only love. She'd met him when she was just a kid and had loved him from that day on.

The house was finished except for the laundry, which she was bundling up to take to the laundromat. Next she'd fix the picnic lunch they'd have on the beach while she ran back and forth to the laundromat just off the beach.

The children had been playing quietly all morning—a little nagging about 'when are we going to the beach' as usual, but otherwise peaceful.

Suddenly the peaceful atmosphere ended. All four children were shrieking.

Janie flew to the door. "Alligator!" came to her panicked mind. She grabbed open the door and shook her head in disbelief. "Janna!" she called out, running across the porch, shrieking herself.

"How did you find us?" she asked as kids hung themselves over her sister's body.

Janna drug them along with her like four giggling leeches. She leaned over to kiss Janie on the cheek, her fingers tangled into Janie's hair and she tugged, laughing impishly.

Janie laughed as she remembered how Janna used to aggravate her that way. Janie had been very controlled and Janna had often delighted in driving Janie into fits of anger when they were kids. Now she did it to tease her. She still loved to walk past Janie and yank her hair.

"I'll die bald!" Janie protested, her thick auburn hair shining with health.

Janna's little red convertible was packed. Books spilled over the narrow jumpseat. Colorful bags tucked everywhere between bags and clothing. A rear luggage rack carried a pile of luggage and a bicycle clung to the back bumper. Two fluffy little dogs hung their heads over the passenger door looking in wonder at the kids.

Janie looked at her car. "Are you coming or going?" she asked.

"Coming!" Janna said as she opened the door to let the dogs bounce out. The dogs were immediately engulfed with kids. They knew Muffy and Puffy. Janna had carted them around with her for years. Before them, there had been others—cats, dogs, everything but children.

"I came to see you in Iowa and had to chase after you down here!" Janna laughed, swinging back her long bronzed hair.

"What happened to the south of France?' Janie asked.

Janna made a face and glanced toward the kids. "Tell you later, sis," she said, a shadow crossed her lively hazel eyes, "when I can talk about it."

Janie kissed her cheek. "I'm glad you're here," she said.

Janie and her family had always been there for Janna when her world went sour, and when she'd healed she'd leave as suddenly as she had come.

"Home for a fix of safety and of the certain love of the family; a time for Janna to heal," Janie thought.

Janie caught Janna's hand, "You'll love it here, Janna. There's something special about this house and this island."

"It must be special to draw you away from Iowa," Janna laughed, for she'd tried numerous times to send air line tickets to Janie and the family to join her at various places about the world and there'd always been excuses.

"I don't know what got into me," Janie said, "but I've never been happier. The children are as brown as Indians, and even Jake is wearing cut off jeans and fishing with the locals. He's catching dinner now. You probably passed him as you crossed the bridge. He's involved in learning about aqua-culture of oysters. A farmer to the bone whether it's seeding fields of wheat, corn and beans, or the sea. Some very interesting things are going on here with the oyster fisherman and politics and Jake is fascinated."

Janna looked around downstairs. The back porch in particular delighted her. "Could I sleep here?" she asked, plumping down on a nest of pillows on the old army cot turned daybed.

"If you really want to," Janie answered, "though we have plenty of room upstairs."

Everyone helped unpack Janna's car. The little dogs ran around frantically trying to keep up with everyone.

Soon Janna's luggage was stowed away. Books spilled over the table and piled up beside the daybed. Bright packages and unwrapped items were pulled from bags.

"Didn't get these wrapped," she said, tossing each person things she'd accumulated for them over a period of months.

Janna's homecomings were always this way. Her gifts could be anything, but each gift was sure to be well selected for the person it went to.

"Oh! Gracious!" Janie exclaimed as Jakie was given a magician's cape, hat and magic kit.

"We'll have white rabbits everywhere!" Alicia teased.

Jake came in just as the kids scampered off, dogs flying at their heels, to put their gifts in their rooms.

"Supper's here!" he called out. He and Janie exchanged glances as he hugged Janna. "Hello, bad penny," he said softly. Janna put her head on his shoulder and he patted it as though she were one of the kids. "I'm glad you're here," he said. Somewhere in her travels Janna had found him a pair of bright red overalls.

The family walked Janna to the beach after supper.

The moon was a perfect half circle—it threw moonbeams of silvery light. "It's so quiet here," Janna mused. "France was so NOISY—it was never serene." She watched the dance of the silvery light on the dark waters.

*

After the family went to bed that night, Janna sat in the stillness of the house. Night noises of frogs and insects were the only sounds anywhere. She lay on the daybed propped up on big pillows and tried to read. She finally lay down the book after realizing she had read the same chapter several times. Her little dogs looked up at her when she moved to sit on the swing. She patted the seat beside her and they hopped up, snuggling close by her side. She patted their heads and they fell back to sleep.

Janna was hurt—really wounded. Reading was usually a good escape from reality but it wasn't happening.

She tried to block out his face, to blot away the cruel harsh lines beside his sensual mouth. The memory of his thick black hair and flashing eyes filled her mind. There was no escaping the memories. Her eyes sought the silhouette of the vine-shrouded trees outside the house. She saw the glimmer of the moon on the bay and thought of the Mediterranean. She gave up and let him come into her head. She let the heartache flood her soul as she moved from the swing and fell facedown on the daybed, smothering the sobs she'd held back since France.

She was safe now, she could cry. No one was here to mock her, taunt her pain. She was home.

She must have slept, for he no longer tortured her mind; a gentle hand reached to dry her tears. Tender lips brushed hers, and arms cradled her close.

Her pain was gone. All scars of the past healed and became nothing, for she was home and he was with her for forever.

Janna slept. Her lips curved in a smile. Her heart sang.

\*

Janna woke up to the sound of the family shushing each other to be quiet so she could sleep. She smiled at the efforts. They were all so dear to her. She had slept so well. It had been such a long time since she'd felt such peace. She stretched and lay awhile longer listening to the family. She heard Janie send the children out to play and then heard them come to the back window and peek in to see if she was awake yet. She opened her eyes and made a face at them. They screeched with joy and ran back around the house and in the door. "She's awake! She's awake!" she heard them shouting to Janie just before they tore through the door and jumped up on the bed with her. "We let you sleep!" they said.

Janie came in with a cup of coffee and shooed them away. She handed the cup to Janna. "Did you sleep well?" she asked.

"Like I was in heaven," Janna answered.

Janie went back in to the kitchen and brought out a cup of coffee for herself.

She and Janna sat side by side on the swing.

Janie sat silently listening to Janna chatter. Bright, sometimes wacky pieces of her life fell (it would seem randomly to anyone but Janie) from her lips in abbreviation of her life.

Janna could tell the funny side of her life— could make you roll with laughter. Janie knew that her sister's flip, often careless chatter was often a cover up for sadness. Her playgirl façade was the only way she knew to cope. She ran, she danced, laughed—elusive as mercury. When the fanciful worlds she entered collapsed, she ran. She left doors open so she'd have space to run, but when the ultimate pain came—the pain that running couldn't cure— she came to Janie and somehow, together, they pieced her back together again.

Janna was a moth who flew too close to the flame of life. She wanted it all but found herself with nothing. Her heart had been flushed with the frequency of a commode. Her dreams had gone down the drain all over the world.

Over the last couple of years Janie and Jake had been aware of a sort of fatigue that Janna pushed herself past. "One day," they said, "she'll come home to stay." It was a hope, not a real belief.

Janie watched Janna chatter more than she listened. "She's better today than she was yesterday," Janie thought.

She was suddenly aware that she'd been asked a question.

"I'm sorry, what did you say?" she asked.

Janna laughed. "Tuning me out?" she teased.

"No, tuning you IN," Janie replied; their eyes met. "Now, the question again?"

"You're going to think this is silly," Janna said, "but I dreamed about a man and the man I dreamed of was the man I've loved forever. Someone so special he could never exist, but still someone I know deep in my heart. I know this sounds nuts, Janie, but he came to me here last night and today I'm happy. I feel him still. The anguish of yesterday is just GONE. I feel peace, maybe for the first time ever." Janna turned a happy face toward Janie. A soft sheen of tears glazed her eyes. "Somehow I'm well of everything that ever happened. I'm home."

Janie could feel her heart beat in her throat. "Janna," she took her sister's hand, "I understand more than you can know. There's SOMETHING going on here. I've not had the courage to talk to Jake or really even to admit it to myself. I'm home here, too; and there's more. Come with me."

Janie stood up, "Come with me," she said, drawing Janna up to stand beside her.

Janie led her up the stairs, pausing half way up. "Look," she said.

Janna leaned forward. Her fingers caressed the faint words carved in the banister. She leaned down to tenderly kiss the names. "David," she whispered. "That's him, I think," she said and followed Janie up the stairs.

"You haven't been to our bedroom," Janie said. "I want you to see it."

The door was closed. Janie always closed it during the day. The hallway was dim and cool.

Janie opened the door and Janna squinted past the sudden rush of sunlight. She stepped forward, standing in the middle of the room. Suddenly she cried out, "No! No! Please don't lock the door! Let me out!" She rushed past Janie. Her eyes were wild as she ran sobbing down the stairs.

Janie caught her as she tried to pull open the heavy front door. "Janna!" she screamed, "Janna!"

Her sister looked around; her eyes were wild and tormented. Tears washed down her face.

Janie reached out and cradled her sister in her arms. Janna sobbed as though her heart were broken.

Janie led her back to the daybed on the porch. She held her as Janna shuddered back the tears. "Now can we talk about it?" Janie asked.

"Something terrified me in that room," Janna said. "For some irrational reason, I thought you were locking me in, and David—the man who came to me in my dreams—I thought he was dead. I thought the sweet love I'd found in his arms was over. What in the hell is this all about?" Janna asked angrily.

Janie's face was white. Her hand clutched her stomach as the babies gave a strong kick in her gut.

"Oh! Lord, Janie! I'm sorry," Janna apologized in alarm. Her hand reached out to soothe Janie's bulging stomach. "Has this hurt the babies—or you?"

Not having experienced pregnancy herself, Janna always envisioned her sister as being as fragile as an egg when she was carrying a child.

"They're just KICKING, Janna! I think they're excited, too!" She looked at Janna and asked, "Do you feel differently about the house now?"

Janna thought for a moment before answering, "No and yes. I feel I belong here, whatever is going on. What about your room, Janie, how does it affect you?"

"I'm drawn to it," Janie replied, "but I can't curtain the window, much as you can't close the door. It suffocates me. The real estate lady who sold us the house said there was a lot of history attached to this place. I never thought a lot about it until today. I think I'd like to find out."

"Let's do," Janna agreed.

*

The next morning Janie and Janna dropped by the real estate office to see Debbie. Jake took the kids fishing and left Janie free to show Janna around the island.

"There's an old lady you could talk to if she's having one of her lucid days," Debbie said.

Debbie seemed to hesitate before asking, "Are you having—uh—problems with the house?"

"Oh, no, quite the contrary—we love it," Janie assured her.

Debbie looked around relieved. "Good luck with Flonzie. She used to know more about the history of this area than any book you could find. Rumors are one thing, but Flonzie knows the facts."

Janie and Janna crossed to the mainland. They saw Jake and the children fishing along the bay and blew the horn at them and waved. They turned left at the crosslands and sought out the nursing home, 'Memory Manor'.

They found a nurse behind the desk and asked if it would be possible for them to talk with Miss Flonzie.

"She loves company," they were told. "Let's see how she is today."

They followed her down the hallway. Several elderly people smiled and spoke to them. A high cracked voice shouted out curses down the hallway. "You son of a bitch—stop that! You're hurting me!"

"Oh, oh!" the nurse sighed. "Flonzie!"

They approached a doorway and looked inside.

A nurse's aide was pulling a coverlet over a shriveled form.  She was catching hell all the while she tried to soothe Flonzie into a better mood.

"Flonzie!" the nurse called out.  "For shame!  You've got company and here you are cursing like a sailor!"

"Hell! I AM a sailor!" Flonzie laughed, her sightless eyes searched the shadows.  "Who is it?" she yelled out.

"A couple of ladies want to talk to you about the old Diehl place.  They bought it and someone told them you know more about its history than anyone in the area knows!" she yelled.

Janie and Janna introduced themselves.  Janie told Flonzie how she'd come to buy the place and told her she wanted to know about it's past.

"Got ghosts there!" the old lady cackled.  "Bet you saw them.  That's why you're here!  Nobody can live there.  The ghosts run them off!  One lady, they ran her crazy a few years ago.  Can't sell the place to anybody around here.  Where're you from?"

"Iowa," Janie smiled.

"Iowa?  Well—you'll be goin' back."

Janie and Janna exchanged glances.  "Tell us about the ghosts," Janie urged gently.

"My mother told me about some of it.  This man from up east, he was a big shot merchant.  His girls were too good for the boys here.  His wife didn't mix neither.  Sent one of the girls away to a boarding school—or so they said. Folks rumored she got in the family way.  Mamma's great grandmother was livin' then.  The girl that was left behind almost grieved herself to death; got so skinny and sick her

61

mother took her off for a cure. Nobody ever came back. The Papa had some ships and he went down on one in a shipwreck a few years later. After that the house was sold and has been steady sold since. Nobody can live around those ghosts. There's a graveyard out back and the stones were never marked. Two graves. Nobody ever knew who, if anybody, lies in those graves. The first buyers were natives, but after that it was sold only to out of state people, or people from further away in Florida. It's been years since anybody tried to live there. People hear things and they see things. Some people the ghosts hated so much they didn't even make it for one night in that house." She seemed to sink into her pillow, "I'm tired now," she said. "I got to pee!" she yelled out. "Call that ugly bitch in here—I got to pee!" she yelled.

Janna stuck her head out the door. She beckoned a passing aide. "She needs a bedpan," she said.

Janie leaned over and kissed Flonzie's forehead. "Thank you!" Flonzie yelled in her face. "I love you," Janie said.

"I love you, too!" Flonzie yelled. "Come back and tell me when you start seeing ghosts!"

"I will," Janie promised.

Janie and Janna thanked the nurse and left. They didn't speak as they walked toward the car. Neither of them was superstitious, but given the circumstances they each wondered in their own minds if, indeed, the house wasn't haunted.

As she backed out of the parking lot Janna looked over at Janie. "Ghosts?" Janna wondered. "Do you think I'm in love with a ghost?"

They laughed.

"Weren't you always?" Janie asked gently.

"Yeah, I suppose so. It's like that song—'I chase the bright elusive butterfly of love' and my luck—I caught a ghost!"

"I always heard that if you ask a ghost who they are and what they want, they'll tell you and then leave you alone," Janie said.

"I don't want the one who kissed me last night to EVER leave me alone!" Janna replied.

"Janis and David forever," Janie said softly. "I wonder who they were."

*

That night after the family went to bed, Janna tried to read. The south of France was pretty much forgotten as far as the pain went, but ghosts and ghost kisses obscured the print on the pages. She finally put the book down. She found her canvas shoes and left the house quietly.

She threaded her way down the pathway to the beach. The moonlight turned the sand to silver and joined the waves of the gulf in ripples of light. The waves were lively and tipped with silver. They almost sounded like music as they danced to and fro along the silver sand.

Janna started for the waters. Her hands were working her tee shirt up about her bare breasts when the bark of a dog caused her to hesitate.

She was startled to see a head bobbing across a silvery path in the water. A big dog leaped beside it like a porpoise.

Janna sat beside a clump of sea oats between small dunes and watched the two frolic in the silver tipped waves. It was like watching water ballet. Janna smiled happily.

After some time the two came ashore.

Janna hadn't known whether the person with the dog was male or female. It was like an unveiling to see the tall, slender, form of a man emerge from the water.

The moonlight outlined his slender body; his buttocks shone white as his body blended with the dusky night.

The dog shook furiously.

The man reached up to smooth back his hair. His body curved backward and moonlight cast his body in silver.

"Adonis!" Janna thought as her heart quickened. "I feel like a voyeur."

The naked man in the moonlight was the most beautiful, exciting man she'd ever seen. She wanted to strip off her clothes and run naked to join him, but of course, she couldn't.

"What an island!" she thought with a smile. "Last night I let a ghost make love to me, and tonight I'm spying on a naked native!"

Suddenly she gave a start. She'd been watching the wonderful play of moonlight on the man's body. The dog was racing toward her! She was frozen. She didn't know whether to jump up and run or stay put. Her muscles bunched and a voice called "Wad!" The dog turned toward the call. "Wad!" the man called again slapping his hands together and the dog ran to him. They walked off down the beach.

Janna watched until the night swallowed them up, the man still naked. There had been no clothes in sight. He had walked away naked. "To where?" Janna wondered. She would have loved to walk along naked beside him and his dog. "Am I so desperate?" she wondered and thought, "No, it's nothing like that."

A magical thing had happened—to a man, a dog, and a woman but only the woman and the dog knew.

Janna slept softly as a woman sleeps who's been loved.

\*

After breakfast was cleared away the next morning, the kids and Jake left for the beach.

Janna helped Janie straighten the house. She made no attempt to go near Janie's bedroom though she was curious as to what effect it might have on her. "I'm too mellow to get screwed up," she thought.

"See any ghosts?" Janie had asked her that morning.

"Nope, you?" Janna laughed.

"This mob has probably scared them away," Janie answered, gathering up an armload of laundry. "I HATE going to that hot laundromat!" Janie arched her back. "These babies are getting heavier to tote around everyday."

"I'll do the laundry," Janna offered, then insisted.

"I think we'll shop for a washer/dryer combo tomorrow," Janie decided. "Want to go to the big city tomorrow?"

"Not really," Janna said, "unless you need me. I've had enough of big cities. I could babysit."

"Maybe we'll take the kids," Janie said. "There's a big goofy-golf course and water slide we promised to let them do before we go back to Iowa. You can rest, Janna."

"Okay," Janna agreed, "but today I do laundry."

*

Janna filled the large washers and put in the coins. The laundromat was hot and humid. The large sign proclaiming to be a 'Watering Hole' beckoned.

She left the laundry and went down the boulevard to the bar and grill. The air inside was cool and a jukebox played the latest popular hit.

A pretty blonde lady smiled from the behind the bar. "Hi!" she was greeted as soon as she walked through the door.

The 'Watering Hole' consisted of a bar, a few tables, the jukebox and some video game machines. A smell of something good came from the kitchen through the door behind the bar.

A tall lean man sat talking to the blonde. He wore a pair of cut off jeans and his feet were bare except for a pair of plastic thongs.

Janna ordered a Miller Lite. The man called out 'JOAN!' and the blonde looked around and let out a shriek.

Janna clutched the bar. The man held a pistol aimed at the blonde. Janna's heart lurched as Joan grabbed under the bar and came out with another pistol. Water shot out across the bar both ways. Joan had ducked to get her pistol. The man had missed but she hadn't. The man's face streamed with water. Janna laughed nervously.

She gathered that the man was called 'Hoyt' and that he and Joan obviously knew each other well.

Joan came over to Janna. "You'll have to overlook us," she laughed.

"You had me going there for awhile," Janna said. "I thought those pistols were real for a moment!"

"I'm sorry," Joan apologized, her eyes large and anxious.

Hoyt laughed and soon they were all chatting.

Janna found out that Hoyt and his friend David had helped Jake unload the U-Haul and move into the Diehl house.

"David, that name again," Janna thought. "I heard the house is haunted," Janna said.

"That's what the people say," Hoyt answered. "I know that David said his arms prickle every time he goes near the house. There have always been stories and people around here believe them. That's why no one knows who's buried over there. No record, they say, just two graves."

Janna shivered. She finished the last of her Miller and rose to leave. "I'd better go put my laundry in the dryer," she said.

"Come back while it dries. We promise not to shoot!" Joan laughed her loud raucous laugh.

Janna liked her. "Okay," she agreed.

She thought of the house as she loaded the laundry into the dryers and walked back over to the 'Watering Hole'.

When Janna returned, Hoyt had left his seat to play a video game at the back of the room.

A tall, thin man in cut off jeans stood at his elbow, a cigarette in one hand and a Budweiser in a 'huggie' in the other. They were both intent on the game.

Joan saw her looking at the two men.

"They play Ms. Pac Man almost everyday. She's their woman."

Janna laughed, "Are you jealous of her?"

"I would be if she had tits!" Joan shot back then placed her hand over her mouth. Her big blue eyes laughed. "My mouth keeps me in trouble!" The man beside Hoyt put down his beer, stubbed out his cigarette and reached up to push back his hair.

Janna's breath caught. She felt a slow blush creep over her face. "Is that David?" she asked Joan.

"Yeah, would you like to meet him?" Joan asked and without waiting for an answer she called out, "David! Come here!"

David walked over. Janna studied his face. His face was small, his cheekbones beautiful, his nose beautiful; a sandy colored mustache covered his upper lip. His lower lip looked full and sweet. His chin was strong, and all over his face there were freckles, their color soft on his tanned skin. "Endearing," Janna thought. "A beautiful endearing face."

Janna wanted to brush back his sun-lightened sandy hair that fell in a fluffy bang over his greenish brown eyes. She knew he was the man she'd watched last night in the moonlight. She blushed again as she met his eyes.

Hoyt came over as they were introduced and they all chatted about the Diehl place.

Janna suddenly remembered the clothes in the dryer. "OH! The laundry!" she laughed, jumping up.

Hoyt and David reached for the fresh beers that Joan put before them. "Nice to meet you," David said. Their eyes met and held for a moment.

Janna walked back to the laundromat thinking of David naked in the moonlight.

That night she wrote for the first time since she'd left Europe. She had feared she was experiencing writers block.

The family was in bed. The porch was quiet and peaceful with only the night sounds outside. The poem came to her as she lay daydreaming on the daybed.  She got up found her laptop computer and wrote:

FAIRIES DANCED ON SILVER SAND


WHEN I THOUGHT ALL WAS GONE
MAGICALLY YOU CAME ALONG
TO TOUCH MY HEART AND DRY MY TEARS
TO HEAL MY SOUL AND QUELL MY FEARS
WHERE I HELD BACK YOU DREW ME OUT
AND TAUGHT ME WHAT LIFE WAS ABOUT

SILVER MUSIC SUNG IN WIND
MAGIC DREAMS BEGAN TO SPIN

MOONLIGHT SHONE UPON YOUR FACE
MY WORLD BEFORE BECAME ERASED
SILVER SAND AND A FROTH TIPPED SEA
ALL THESE THINGS YOU GAVE TO ME

AND FAIRIES DANCED UPON SILVER SAND
MOONBEAMS CUPPED INTO MY HAND
WILD MUSIC FROM A PAGAN REED
FILLED ME WITH ALL THAT I COULD NEED

AND FAIRIES DANCED UPON SILVER SAND
MOONBEAMS GLITTERED IN MY HANDS
MUSIC WAILED FROM A PAGAN WAND
IN A MOONBEAM BED WE WERE ONE

AND FAIRIES DANCED AND MUSIC MOANED
AS MY HEART FOUND WHERE IT BELONGED
MY HEART FOUND WHERE IT BELONGED.

*

The next day Janie, Jake, and the children went to the city.

Janna's mind turned to David more often than she was comfortable with. She was restless.

After pacing around the house she decided to walk along the beach to clear her head.

She searched for a bathing suit and pulled a long shirt out of one of her suitcases.

The beach was practically deserted. "I guess the tourists aren't up yet," she thought as though she weren't one.

She pulled off her canvas shoes and walked along the water's edge. The waves played around her legs. Ghost crabs scurried all around the sand. Tiny seashells washed over her toes. The gulf roared softly as sunshine sprinkled light upon its waves. A soft gulf breeze lifted her hair from her shoulders in gentle puffs.

Janna walked with a happy feeling in her heart and peace in her soul. Perspiration soon beaded her forehead giving her a feeling of robust health. She sprinted along the waters edge. Seagulls moved away from her approach. She frolicked with the heart of a child. A sense of freedom carried her high. Janna hadn't noticed how far she'd come until she glanced over to see she was almost across from the 'Watering Hole'. She realized that she was thirsty.

Joan was behind the bar. Hoyt and David were absent. A couple of tourists sat at the bar having some of the hair of the dog that had bitten them the night before. Hangover was written all over them. A young couple sat at a small table in the back.

Joan called out "Hi!"

Janna slid onto a stool. "Want something to drink?" Joan asked.

"I didn't bring any money along," Janna said. "I didn't expect to walk this far."

"That's okay, you can put it on a tab," Joan offered.

"Okay. Miller Lite," Janna said.

Janna and Joan chatted for awhile as Joan wiped down the counter.

The door opened and a raspy, loud voice called out, "Hello, Darling!" to Joan. A girl walked in trailed by a chubby Cuban-looking boy. Her hair was a mess, mascara smudged under her eyes and she appeared to be wearing nothing under a thigh high long tee shirt and it was none too clean. She ordered a beer and talked loudly to the men at the bar. She was obviously drunk although the day was young.

She pushed a soda toward the kid. He had an overgrown look. He was probably much younger than his size indicated.

The girl's name was apparently Martha.

A couple of guys came in and she hugged them. Her tee shirt had worked up revealing half a hip with no panties in sight.

Janna looked away. She'd seen girls like her before.

Martha was laughing uproarishly.

Soon she and the two guys left together. The kid trailed along in silence.

"Put that on David's tab," she called out to Joan. One of the guys snickered.

"David?" Janna asked.

"She's David's girlfriend," Joan said. "They're suppose to get married this weekend."

Something happened to Janna's heart. "He seemed so NICE," Janna said.

"He is," Joan agreed.

"Then WHY?" Janna asked unable to find the words.

Joan rolled her eyes. "He's had some rotten luck lately—maybe he's just given up. She's a slut—there's nothing she doesn't do. Last

71

night she had sex with two guys on the beach. She's screwing her ass off, even with David's friends. He should know by now."

Janna's heart had shriveled in sadness. The joy she'd felt on the beach died. "So he's getting married this weekend," she said just to hear it again.

\*

Janie, Jake and the kids came home in high spirits. They'd had a great time at the goofy golf course, water slide and amusement park.

They had also bought a washer and dryer, which was to be delivered the next day.

No one noticed Janna's silence.

The family finally ran down and everyone went to bed early. After Janna collected her goodnight kisses, she sat on her daybed to read.

The book blurred as her thoughts overpowered the text.

She thought of taking a walk and then decided 'no'. "Hell, next I'll be seeing HER naked in the moonlight screwing like a dog in the sand!" Janna stood up impatiently. Paradise—her Shangri-La—had developed a twist of bitterness. She had that old feeling back again, the feeling that said 'RUN!'

She didn't want to run, not now, but she knew she would. She felt an enveloping sadness. She paced back and forth for awhile and then went to the kitchen.

She dug around in the pantry until she found the bottle of gin she knew was in there somewhere with a couple of other bottles kept out of the reach of the children. Neither Janie nor Jake drank hard liquor, beyond an occasional highball and then it was only after the children were in bed.

She found some gin and tonic water. There were no limes so she splashed in a few drops of real lemon. She'd fixed a tall glass of the drink and ice cubes. She stared morosely at the cold clear ice as she brought the drink to her lips. "Maybe I'll sleep," she thought, desiring escape from the day she'd suffered through.

At last, south of France came back to ravage her mind and heart. She cried in her sleep. In the twilight of the room her lover came and she turned her back on him. She felt him standing there beside her and suddenly he was gone.

Her dreams were strange. There was death and torment and tragic agonizing heartbreak. Suddenly a searing pain ripped through her body and she woke up with a scream on her lips. She heard footsteps running down the stairs and thought she was with them. Janie and Jake burst onto the porch.

Janie turned on the light.

Janna sat up in the bed trying to remember what had happened. She could still hear the echo of a scream in her head and knew it must have been hers.

"It was a crazy dream," she reassured Janie and Jake.

Janie watched her eyes. "Want me to sit with you for awhile?" she asked.

"For awhile," Janna answered.

"Was it just a dream?" Janie asked after Jake had gone to bed.

"Yes," Janna said. "It sort of was and it wasn't, if you can understand that."

\*

Janis R. Scott

The next morning the washer and dryer were delivered.

"I'll get a plumber to hook this up," Jake said.

Janie, Jake and the kids were going to fish. They asked Janna to come along.

She felt listless. "I think I'll just rest," she said. "Besides, if you are lucky enough to get a plumber out today, someone will have to be here."

After the family left Janna lay back on the daybed. A breeze drifted through the screen behind the open windows. A bug buzzed outside trying to push it's way in.

Janna looked out through the tangle of vegetation to the bay. "God, it's beautiful here," she groaned and wanted to reclaim her previous joy. She dozed off listening to the insects drone. A loud knocking on the front door awoke her.

She hurried to the door expecting the family to be back from fishing.

She opened the door to find David standing there.

Her mouth felt dry. She stared.

"I'm here to see what I'll need to hook up the washer and dryer," he said.

Janna opened the door. She thought of his body in the moonlight and imagined him lying beside the coarse, crude girl called Martha. Her God of the moonlight shouldn't have feet of clay. It wasn't fair. Something beautiful had been defiled.

David told her that Jake had seen him driving down the street and hailed at him. He had told him what he needed done and that Janna would be there.

There was nothing for Janna to say. She tried to say something pleasant about the weather, then left to go back to the porch. She picked up a book and pretended to herself that she was reading.

She heard David moving about inside and outside the house. He came to the doorway of the porch before he left.

She saw him quickly scan her stack of books.

"Yours?" he asked.

"Yes," she replied.

"I love to read," he said.

"So do I," she said looking into his beautiful green-gold eyes.

"How could he?" she asked herself again.

David came early the next morning. "I have another job after I finish here," he explained.

He unloaded PVC pipe, various fittings and tools. Janna heard the sound of shoveling and a shiver ran over her body. She found herself rushing to the door of the porch.

David stood outside. His back was toward as he bent over to lift a shovel of sand and shell. She could see the sweat gleaming on his brown back. He wore only a pair of cut offs and shoes. The cut offs were short and ragged. She studied his body as he worked. There was a dearness about him that touched her heart. She turned her eyes away only to feast them on him again.

"I couldn't be falling in love with this island boy," she thought. "This island *man*," she corrected herself.

She thought of the jet set, suave types she'd known and had come to loathe. The contrast was glaring.

"Maybe I'm only running from them," she mused, "but," her heart said, "there's a strong attraction for this man. An attraction like you've never felt before." Janna knew it was true.

"This weekend," her heart reminded her. "This weekend and he's forever beyond reach. He's walking into folly and you're running again."

A tear slid down Janna's face. She looked up to see David at the door.

"Could I come this way?" he asked.

Janna quickly brushed aside the tear. She could smell the faint odor of his body as he passed by. It was good to smell a man smell. It aroused her as one animal's scent arouses another. Her heart beat fast. She WANTED him. She wanted to hold him, to kiss him. And then WHAT ELSE? she wondered, not being able to look further.

She heard a scamper of feet on the front porch and the children burst in. They immediately assaulted David with questions and with tales of their fishing.

Janna noticed how genuinely he seemed to enjoy the kids. They wanted to pet his dog. He went outside with them.

Janie and the children were headed for the beach. "We're trying to soak up as much sun as we can. We don't have much longer to stay," Janie laughed.

Janna realized with a start that they would all be leaving the island in a few days. "So WHY am I concerning myself with this David?" she asked herself and shrugged as she turned away from looking through the window at him playing with the dog and the children.

The children urged her to come to the beach with them after Janie had fixed them lunch. "Maybe later," she'd said.

David reappeared and began to move the washer toward the wall where he'd put in fittings.

"I'll help you," Janna offered and pushed the opposite side closer to the connections.

"You're strong!" he laughed.

"VERY," Janna replied, looking into his heart-stopping eyes.

Her heart moved her with no mind involved as she stepped around the washer to face him. He looked into her eyes as she spoke. "David, you don't know me, and this is none of my business, but Martha's not the person for you. I don't know WHO is, but it's NOT her."

David's eyes withdrew like a curtain pulled shut. The lights in his eyes extinguished and dully slid away from Janna's searching look.

Something in Janna pushed her further. It was now or never she knew. It HAD to be said, though she suspected nothing could or would be changed. She HAD to say the words to him. "DAVID," she called back his eyes. "David?" she took a deep breath. Her heart was resolved and she knew the audacity with which she spoke.

"David, this is a good way to get AIDS—she's having sex with EVERYONE indiscriminately. She's even having sex with your 'friends'. According to some people who know, this week there were two guys during the course of one night. They each had her on the beach."

David seemed shrunken. "WHY HER?" Janna asked.

"Someone to sleep with," David said quietly. His freckles seemed to stand out in relief from his pale face.

"You CAN'T be that desperate," Janna pursued, and standing there she knew, she wanted him for herself!

Janna felt the sluttish girl had tainted him. She felt sorry for the wretched look she'd brought to his face.

They stood there facing each other. Each was lost in their own anguish. Their eyes were closed against contact. The curtains drawn against the other's seeing what lay behind.

A knock at the door broke into some sort of stalemate.

The words had been said, they'd been heard.

Janna walked to open the door. Hoyt smiled at her. "David here?" he asked in his abrupt way.

Janna changed her face. She smiled pleasantly. "Yes, come in!" she said, "If you've left that water gun at home, that is!"

Hoyt had brought a fitting from the hardware store on the mainland. They worked together to finish the job. Janna sat in the porch staring out toward the bay. She felt she was in some sort of limbo. She heard the men's voices outside as they worked.

When the job was finished David came to the door. He looked into Janna's eyes for a long moment then turned and walked down the steps.

Janna stood in the open doorway watching them drive away. David didn't look back and she wondered what he was thinking.

*

Janie and Janna spent the next day together.

"Have you seen any ghosts, yet?" Janie asked.

"Not really," Janna replied, "but I FEEL things here."

"So do I," Janie said, "There's something UNRESOLVED—something compelling. I can't even describe my feelings about this place. I actually hate to leave and yet Iowa is our home. My heart is torn between there and here. Jake likes it here, for a vacation, but he's already antsy to get back to the farm. We'll be going in three days, Janna. Will you be coming with us?"

"Three days," Janna thought. "So little time—so little time to do WHAT," she wondered. "Hang around and see David get married?"

"I'll follow you guys back," she said, "but strangely enough I don't want to leave either."

"If you can handle the solitude, you're more than welcome to stay. No one will be coming for sometime yet and it would be good to have someone staying here, though I'd love to have you with us."

"Solitude is no stranger to me, Janie," Janna answered quietly. "No matter who I'm with I'm usually alone, unless it's with you, Jake and the kids. I've never really felt I belonged anywhere actually. That's why it's so strange that I feel that belonging here."

Janie hugged Janna, "I know, honey," she said. Janna was the other half of her heart.

\*

Janna made it through the next day without seeing David. Whether to stay or go to Iowa was uppermost in her mind. She was torn.

Janie and Janna talked and she knew she could confide anything to Janie but she held back her senseless attachment to David. She even walked up the stairs and sat beside the worn old carving half way up the stairs. Her fingers reached for the banister and gently traced David, David, David. To her it meant the David who had trespassed where no other man ever had—where no one else had been allowed. The David, who had unknowingly, innocently, trod upon her heart.

"I'll have to go," Janna decided. A draft of icy air brushed past her like a shove. Janna shivered and looked over her shoulder.

Nothing stirred. "My imagination," she said, the hair on her arms still bristled as she rubbed away the sensation.

*

The next day was a day of packing for the early morning departure on the following morning.

Janna put off stowing away her possessions she'd brought. Her carefree lifestyle and frequent travels had made packing easy. She felt she could do it in her sleep. Her books took up a lot of the space in her small car. Her little dogs and their blankets and toys took up as much. The suitcases she strapped on the back and had not been fully unpacked. She kept her few cosmetics and a small overnight bag in the car. Her bicycle was still unused since she'd arrived at the island.

The family had numerous suitcases building up by the front door.

That night the family went to bed early. The station wagon was packed.

Janna was restless. She picked out a pair of shorts and a shirt, pulled a pair of sneakers she'd already packed out of her bag and dressed quietly.

She left the house walking toward the small scattering of buildings that served the island as their business section.

The long walk was like a goodbye to the sound of the gulf. It's soft roar pulsing like blood coursing in her veins. It was goodbye to the night sounds, the soft wind, the scent of the verdant vegetation mingling with the heady scent of the wind blowing over the tangy waters of the gulf. It was a sad sense of farewell that she felt as she walked slowly toward the little gulf-side village.

Several cars lined the street in front of the 'Watering Hole'. David's big truck was one of them. Wad lay in front of the truck possessively.

As Janna approached the door David stepped out. Their eyes met.

Janna turned to walk beside him to the truck. It seemed a natural thing to do.

He turned to face her when he reached the truck.

"I wanted to apologize for being so tactless," Janna said. "It was none of my business."

"You embarrassed me," he said quietly.

"I'm sorry," Janna apologized feeling embarrassed herself.

"No," David said. "You embarrassed me and I've broken off the relationship. People had tried to tell me. I guess I knew. I don't think there would have been a wedding. It was her idea and I just hadn't protested. I think I'd given up."

"So are you okay?" Janna asked.

"Yes," he replied looking into her eyes. "Are you folks leaving tomorrow?" he asked.

"Yes, but I may stay on for another week after they go. I write but I've not been writing for awhile. I think I'd like to begin again. This is such a beautiful peaceful place I find the creative juices beginning to flow again."

David's interest piqued. "What do you write?"

"Fiction," Janna replied. "Some psychological mystery, some romance, whatever comes into my head and turns into a book."

"It sounds fascinating," David said.

"Sometimes it is and sometimes it's just work. I think I could enjoy writing here."

"Then why don't you just STAY here?" David asked.

"I don't know; maybe someday," Janna said wistfully.

"If I give you my address, will you drop me a few lines now and then?" David asked.

"If you'll write, too," she smiled, wondering what sort of letter the island man would be likely to write.

"I'm not sure where I'll be," Janna said, adding, "but how could I contact you to give you an address when I'm settled?"

"Here at the 'Watering Hole'," David answered. "The post office delivers my mail here." He gave Janna the box number and she carefully committed it to memory.

\*

The family left early the next morning. Janna watched the kids leave, clutching their individual bags of seashells in one hand and waving frantically from the windows as they drove off.

She stood alone with the house. The soft roar of the gulf murmured in her ears, cries of birds broke the monotony of the soothing sounds of the surging waters. The gardenia bushes had never smelled so sweet as their perfume joined the natural scent of the gulf and jungle-like vegetation of the island.

Janna walked back into the house. It felt so right. Her restless heart felt at peace.

She poured a cup of coffee and took it to the back porch. The sunroom was bathed in soft sunlight. She sat on the swing gently swinging to and fro as she sipped her coffee. She was at peace.

She finished the coffee and took the cup to the sink. Her eyes traveled toward the stair and she smiled.

When she returned to the sun porch, she picked up her yellow legal pad. All she'd written since she'd come to the island and for some period of time before, since France, had been the poem.

She found a pen and her hand began to fly over the pages.

A story had begun to tantalize her mind since she'd reached the island. She knew part of it and the rest would 'just happen' as she wrote. She was back to herself—she was doing the only thing that gave her satisfaction other than her family.

She wrote all morning. The words spilled from her pen. She put down the pad to have a light lunch and began again. The story was taking form. Janna was excited to be able to begin giving it birth. It had been germinating in her brain too long—it had to come out.

By four o'clock Janna was fatigued. She'd reached a place in her book where she could fork off into two different directions. She wasn't sure which one she wanted to choose. She put down her pad and paced around the room trying to decide which avenue to take. They were both enticing.    She decided to give it a rest.

She showered and pulled on a clean tee shirt and some shorts.    She found her sneakers and took them outside to dump grains of sand out of them.    Her little dogs frisked around her. She knew they missed the kids.    "Okay you little mutts!" she laughed.    "I'll take you for a drive.    I know you like that!"

She opened the door of her little red convertible and they scrambled over each other getting in.    She hadn't taken time to explore the island herself.    She'd taken drives with Janie and the kids and the dogs—all of them crowded into the station wagon and the kids pointing out everything of interest to them. She wanted to slowly and peacefully seek out all the beauty of the island.    Her camera was in the car and she checked it for film.    The dogs looked at her expectantly—they were ready to feel the breeze flying past them as they sped along.

On impulse Janna drove past the 'Watering Hole'.    Joan and Hoyt were just coming out the door and they waved her down.

They were going over to the large bar and grill by the marina for a drink.    "Change of scene!" Joan laughed her rough laugh.    "My friend over there pours them almost triple for us!"

Janna shuddered at the thought.

They urged Janna to come with them.

Janna knew that where Hoyt was David was often there, too.    "I promised these pooches a drive.    They're bored with the kids gone and no one to play with.    How about I drive them around for awhile and get some air myself. I've been in all day and need to blow the cobwebs out of my mind.    I'll drop them back at the house after that and if you're still here I'll join you."

"Oh, we'll probably be here!" Joan laughed.

"See you, then," Janna waved and backed out of the parking space. David's big truck was nowhere to be seen as she drove the eager little dogs up and down the island.

When Janna joined Hoyt and Joan they were well on their way. The triple margaritas must have been forthcoming. Hoyt ordered one for Janna and they laughed at her expression when she took a sip. Their friend hadn't spared the liquor in hers either.

Janna sipped a couple of margaritas while she watched Hoyt and Joan consume several at an alarming rate.

Janna hadn't explored the island as she'd intended. It was getting late for much exploration. She had expected David to come in at some point and he hadn't. Trying to sound casual she had asked about him. "He's probably home reading a book and drinking a few beers," she was told. Janna asked, "Where does he live anyway?"

Hoyt gave a rather detailed description of how to get to David's house. He kept repeating some of it and Janna laughed. She knew Joan and Hoyt were pretty will snookered.

When she got up to leave she realized she was a little tipsy too. She stood a moment beside her barstool. "I'm a little woozy, I think!" she laughed. "How do you guys do it?"

"We practice!" Joan laughed uproarishly.

Janna heard herself giggling. "You okay to drive?" Joan asked. Horrified that Joan would insist on driving her, Janna quickly replied. "Nothing a little fresh air won't cure," and left hurriedly.

The sun was low and a hint of pastel was already beginning to spread through the clouds. The cloud shadows interspersed with sunlight turned the waters of the gulf into shade upon shade of blue, green, and violet. "This wouldn't be believable if it were put on canvas," Janna thought. She watched for the street that Hoyt had mentioned that would bring her toward the bay. The road she turned on soon became gravel, then the gravel thinned as she made her next turn. The road softened and her little car pulled more slowly. She almost passed the still smaller road that headed toward a marsh. The vegetation pushed at the road until it practically surrendered to the thick vines and heavy shrubbery. The road softened some more and Janna geared down. The car bogged down and came to a stop.

Janna got out to look at her tires. "Stuck in the damned sand!" she moaned.

She tried to back up. The tires spun and dug in deeper. "Oh! Hell!" she yelled at the car. "Hell! Hell! Hell!"

She tried to rock back and forth to escape the sand. Nothing worked and she only buried her car deeper in the sand.

She took her keys out of the ignition and grabbed her purse. It was getting darker under the jungle greenery.

Deep tracks led down the road. The sand humped in the middle of the tracks. Her little car lay on a bed of sand.

She followed the deep sandy ruts. Her shoes filled with sand and grated against her bare feet. Mosquitoes came from nowhere and savagely attacked her bare legs. She beat at them as she ran. "It shouldn't be much further," she thought as she broke free of the heaviest vegetation and saw an island of black grass off to her left. She knew the water wasn't far away. She kept floundering forward in the sand-filled ruts. Dusk was gathering and the mosquitoes were savage. "What if he's not there?" she wondered, "or if I took the wrong road?" she thought in horror.

The sand inhibited her speed. Her breath came in gasps as she ran desperately trying to outrun the mosquitoes.

It seemed an eternity before she saw the tiny wooden house with the big truck sitting outside.

She flew up the stairs and beat on the door. She could see through the glass panel.

David lay on an old couch. He had a book in his hand. His dog Wad got up from where he lay beside him on the floor. He and David got to the door at the same time.

"The mosquitoes are killing me!" Janna said, tears ran down her cheeks.

David opened the door and pulled her inside. "I didn't hear you drive up," he said. He looked at her and smiled. His finger reached out and touched her wet cheek. "You're safe from them now," he said. "They don't like us natives—we're too tough—they wait for tender, sweet meated tourists!"

He looked past her shoulder. "You didn't walk?" he asked in surprise.

"RAN," she said rubbing her legs. She saw David's look of surprise. "I ran from where I got my car stuck in the sand, that is," she explained, frowning at the red blotches and welts the mosquitoes had left.

"Are they still hurting?" David asked.

"Actually they are," she answered.

David pointed toward the couch. "Wait there. I'll get something to help you."

She watched him go to his tiny kitchen at the back of the room. She heard water running and thought, "Well, he does have indoor plumbing." Wad nudged her hand and she reached out to rub his ears. He snuggled closer.

David came back. "Sit down, Wad," he commanded and the dog gave him a baleful look and lay at Janna's feet with an exaggerated sigh. Janna and David laughed.

"He's a real con," David said affectionately.

He placed a saucer of a white powder on the small table before the couch. He dipped a wet cloth into the powder and said, "Here, stretch out your leg." He dabbed the red spots with the mixture and the stinging went away. "Now the other leg," he said and she obeyed. Next he touched the places on her arms and a couple on her neck.

"What was that?" Janna asked.

"Soda," David replied. "It helps neutralize the poison of the sting."

"Thanks, Doc," Janna teased.

"Now, where were you going?" David asked. "Were you coming here?"

"I was just exploring," Janna said, "and I saw Hoyt and Joan and Hoyt mentioned you lived out this way and I decided to explore this way."

"How far away is your car?" David asked.

"It's on the road that comes straight to your house just a little way after the turn off."

"Are you just stuck a little or did you do like the typical tourist does and bury it to the floorboards before you gave up?"

Janna threw up her hands, "You got me dead to rights, partner, I did the 'tourist' bit, I'm afraid."

David laughed. "I'll get it out with my truck," he said, "but I was about to have something to eat. Would you like to fortify yourself with some watermelon?"

"Sounds great," Janna said as he headed for the tiny kitchen once again.

She looked around his room while he clanked dishes and silverware about in the kitchen.

She was surprised to see a set of shelves built into the wall that was brimming with books that were also favorites of hers. She heard a step behind her and turned to see David with huge slices of watermelon. She hadn't realized how thirsty she was until she saw the icy red melon dripping its juices into the large tray he served it on.

"I was admiring your collection of books," Janna said.

David's face lit up. They discussed authors and books as they ate the watermelon.

When the melon was finished David took the rinds outside and threw them off the porch toward the marsh. "For the animals," he explained.

David had been working on a crossword puzzle and it was lying open on the table in front of the couch. Janna picked it up. "Too tough?" she asked.

"Not tough enough," David said, "I got bored with it."

They began to complete it together. It was fun and time passed by swiftly. Janna really didn't care whether they ever got her car out of the sand. She was strangely happy here in the rickety little house on the edge of the

swamp.     The   man,   David,   held   a   strong
fascination for her.

He may have sensed her mood for he put down
the crossword puzzle they had just completed
and looked at her over his half-glasses.

"We could get the car out in the morning,"
he said.   "You could sleep over there—it's my
bed," he said pointing toward a small bed
built into the room.   "I'd sleep on the couch.
I fall asleep here a lot, anyway."

Janna had no hesitation.   She felt shy but
she knew this was what she wanted to do.

Wad got up and went to the door.   He looked
at David.     "He's ready for his nightly
rounds," David said.

"Will he come back in?" Janna asked.

"Yes, I don't want him out overnight; there
are alligators out there in the swamp and they
like dogs."

Janna thought of her little dogs.   They were
on the porch and probably on her daybed.   She
always kept newspaper near the door in case
they couldn't wait until she got back when she
left them alone which was rare.   They were
almost constant companions.   "I'll have to
watch my little ones more carefully now the
kids are gone.   They stayed around the yard
and played with them on the beach.   They may
get bored and stray now."

"That might be a good idea." David agreed
and asked, "Are they in your car?"

"No," Janna said.   "I took them for a drive
and left them off.   They have water and food
and a newspaper to go on if they can't wait."

She glanced around asking, "Do you have a
bathroom I could use?"

"Right through that door," David pointed to
the door by the bookcase.   "It's not much, but
it's clean."

When Janna came out David handed her a pair of jogging pants and a tee shirt. "I don't have pajamas—maybe these will do," he offered. "It gets cool at night with the wind off the bay. I keep the windows open and the breeze comes in through the screens." He handed her a blanket. "You may need this before morning."

Wad scratched at the door and David let him in. He came over to Janna and nuzzled her. "He likes you," David said.

"He's a good boy," Janna said scratching him. She went back into the bath to change into David's clothes. He was stretched out on the couch as she walked by toward the bed. She leaned over and kissed his cheek. She felt shy and her heart beat swiftly. "Goodnight and God bless you, David," she said softly as she continued on.

"Goodnight," David answered curling up on the couch.

Janna fell asleep sooner than she expected. She knew she wanted to be someone special to David.

The next morning she was awaken by Wad nudging her to wake her up. "Why, hi guy!" she greeted him as he wagged his tail.

She wrinkled her nose and sat up. David was in the kitchen and she could smell bacon frying. "Good morning!" she called out trying to smooth her wild curls.

"I don't have to ask you how you slept!" David called back at her.

"Did I snore?" she asked. "Ask Wad," David laughed. "I slept better than I've slept in a long time myself."

After breakfast David had to go to work. Janna rode in the big truck with him and Wad to drag her car out of the sand.

After the car was out, she followed David to the main road and they waved goodbye and went in opposite directions.

Her little dogs were wild with excitement and jumped all over her. They sniffed her suspiciously after they'd calmed down. They smelled Wad.

Janna let out the dogs and cleaned up the newspaper, which was only wet. She sprayed Lysol around and went to the kitchen to fix coffee.

She called the dogs back in, remembering David's caution about the alligators.

She sat propped up on her big pillow on the daybed and began to write. She attacked the book with new vigor. She knew where she'd take the plot. David haunted her mind, and a key character she hadn't expected stepped upon her pages. David lived another life. The character was him, but not quite him, as his character and personality flowed from the tip of her pen.

Janna wrote feverishly the rest of the week. During this time she saw David twice—each time at the 'Watering Hole' when she'd seen his truck outside and stopped by.

A couple of other times she'd waved to him as he and Wad passed by in their truck and she'd been out driving to the bank or store.

When the day came for her to leave Janna walked along the beach. Telling the island goodbye was strangely hard. She'd told a lot of places goodbye without a backward look.

She savored the sound of the gulf, the funny birds, the waving sea oats on their tall golden stems. She picked up little shells and tucked them in her pocket. They would travel with her. She stood looking out to the horizon and remembered the first night she'd seen David, naked on the beach with Wad playing in the water beside him.

Tears ran down her face as she turned to leave.

The night before she'd seen David at the 'Watering Hole'. She, David, and Joan had chatted. She lingered as long as she could for she needed to get a good night's sleep for the journey ahead—the journey to Iowa and her family.

David walked her to her car. He looked into her eyes. She hoped he'd kiss her, and knew that if he did she couldn't leave.

"Write," he said.

"I will," she promised and left.

He stood watching her drive away. She wanted to turn back.

Janna left the island with tears in her eyes. Her little dogs were eager to ride for they loved to fly along in her little red convertible.

Janna turned the radio loud. Every song reminded her of David.

*

Janie, Jake and the children ran out to meet Janna as she drove up.

It was late in the evening when she arrived.

She'd brought air brushed tee shirts for everyone with various island scenes and the island's name on them.

Everyone was delighted.

Jake was back happily farming. The children were back to their normal routines and Janie and Janna had time to visit.

After a couple of days in Iowa, Janna called Joan at the 'Watering Hole'. She left her address and phone number in Iowa for David.

Several days later a letter arrived from David. Janna opened it immediately. Her heart raced.

The past from the south of France had tried to contact her through her family. She ignored the attempt for nothing was left in her heart but the enchantment of David.

Janna had drawn some cartoons and mailed them to David at the 'Watering Hole'. His letter was a surprise. It was also cute and funny and dear.

"Hi," David opened his letter. He wrote a few paragraphs before saying, "There are so many things I'd like to talk to you about and I'm not sure I should. You seem to trust me as though you've known me forever. I'm really surprised by that."

"There are a lot of things I thought of during the evening you and I spent together at my house. It crossed my mind at least ten or fifteen times that I wanted to—and please take this the way it is meant—

I wanted to kiss you
I wanted to make love to you
I wanted to get to know you
I enjoyed myself
I wondered what you were thinking
I wondered if you wanted to kiss me
I wondered if you wanted to make love to
  me
I also thought to myself that—

When you write back pick an answer—A, H, or all of the above. I believe you and I need a couple of days by ourselves somewhere. First, before we do anything else, let's become friends, then let's be lovers. Both of those are big words and they have every right to be.

I like you and I love your artwork and I think
you are a fine woman and you don't know a damn
thing about me, at all! You know how small
this island is. Things could be said about us
or you or me.

"Janna, you are someone I would like to know
and I mean that. Do you think that in spite
of all the things you have going on in your
life that you could someday spend a couple of
evenings with just me?

"You impress me and I would like to know
you. No promises, just being together and
being you and I!?

"Well, now that I've said all of this I'll
quit and say goodnight. I don't even know any
of your tender spots.

"Wad also said goodnight-slurp! Night,
David."

She let Janie read the letter. Her eyes
widened. "Wow! You're fast!" she laughed,
then a thoughtful look crossed her face.
"DAVID," she said. "Even that's strange—you
know Mother almost named you Janis."

"I thought it was YOU," Janna said.

"No," Janie insisted, "It was you."

"How strange," they agreed. Goosebumps ran
over Janna's arms.

Once Janna had opened the door to
communication about David, his name flowed
from her lips like a babbling brook.

After a couple of days Janie said, "Janna,
sit down and let's talk."

Janna sat.

"Now," Janie said, "all you talk about is
David, David, David, but honey, you're here
and he's there. Isn't that sort of silly?
Are you just infatuated with an idea of David,
or are you genuinely interested in the guy AS
HE IS? He's an islander, lives on the island

and always has.  He'd never be content to travel the globe even if he were financially able to do it, as I'm sure you realize he isn't."

Janna looked at Janie, her expression was sober.  "None of that ever really mattered," she said, "it was just something to do to pass the time."

That night before Janna could sleep she wrote another poem.  She called it KIN.

- Blood to blood we know kin
- Silent spirits meet again
- and with their meeting know
- that kindred blood between them flows.
- Silently without the word
- voices of spirit kin is heard
- Blood to blood as flows the stream
- rivulets make the river teem
- Spirits join with spirits sight
- the strength of kin, the strength of might
- Blood to blood the tide is strong
- Blood to blood and bone to bone.

\*

Janna answered David's letter.  Answering the quiz was fun.  She wrote, "As to your quiz, the answer is E."  Tears of mirth sparkled in her devilish eyes.  She wondered if he'd remember what E was.

A couple of days later Janie said, "Janna, go back to the island—see for yourself what's real and what isn't.  Right now you're living in a world of all fantasy.  You say you love this man and you don't even know him."

"I know him," Janna insisted.

That night she packed.

Muffy, Puffy, and Janna hurried southward toward the island. The little red car drew one speeding ticket and narrowly avoided God knows how many more. The radio blared, the little dogs' ears blew in the wind, as Janna flew down the highway toward her love. She could hardly contain her excitement as she approached the island. Her first stop was at the 'Watering Hole'.

Joan's relief was working. She wasn't there. Hoyt came over to say 'hello'. He said David was working somewhere late. He had a concrete job.

Hoyt bought Janna a beer and she sipped it slowly.

David didn't come and she was tired. She still had the little dogs in the car, she'd been so anxious to let David know she had come back.

She said goodnight and walked to the door. She heard her little dogs barking. She stepped out to see Wad standing beside her car. Her heart gave a leap. Then she saw David. He was walking from his truck. He had his arm around a young girl. Her arm was around him also, as they walked toward the door Janna had just stepped out of.

Janna's dream died. Every sadness she'd ever experienced in her lifetime rolled toward her crushed heart. She reached to open her car door then hesitated. "What the hell!" she said. "I won't run. He'll have to face me at least!"

David and the girl sat at the bar. Her hand rested on his leg. Janna's heart shrunk into a thing of misery. Her tears were held back by sheer willpower. She'd be damned if she'd cry in front of him!

Janna spoke to Hoyt who still sat at the table just behind David. She said, "I decided I would have another beer. Let me buy you one." She motioned to the lady behind the bar. Two beers were opened and held out to them. Hoyt got up to get them.

"You didn't say how long you're here for," Hoyt said.

"I'll be leaving tomorrow for the east," she said regretting the foolhardy trip she'd just made back to the island.

Janna laughed, talked and drank. A couple of Hoyt's friends joined them.

David's back was stiff.

She got very drunk that night. She was alone on the island and her world was blacker than the blackest night.

Janna asked who the girl with David was. She had to know. She was shacking up with David.

Janna felt like a fool. She felt FOOLED and it hurt but she'd traveled that road before—it just had never meant so much as it did now.

Janna felt so down she couldn't force herself to begin the trip the next day.

She and her dogs had driven up to the dark house that night. Janna and the dogs had rushed toward the front door. The dogs may have been expecting the children to be there to greet them. Janna felt like she needed the house for a sanctuary. It still felt like home to her. She grieved for David. She was sick from the beer and sick from her loss.

She woke up with a hangover. It made a good excuse not to leave. She felt so down she couldn't force herself to drive away. She knew she was going—she just couldn't function enough to undertake another long drive. "And a drive to where?" she asked herself. She knew she'd go. In fact, she planned never to see the island again so long as she lived.

The next night Janna found an excuse to go back to the 'Watering Hole'.

David was there. He had a six pack of beer to go.

Janna ignored him. She was angry with him and with herself for being so gullible. Her pride was hurt and her heart was crushed.

David walked to her side. "We've got to talk," he said.

Janna looked into his eyes. "Yes," she said stiffly. She hurt horribly. "WHEN?" she asked.

"How about tomorrow at seven?" David asked.

Janna had to salvage something. Her pride rose above the ashes of her heart. "NO," she said. "NOW—now or never."

"I can't," David said.

"SO?" Janna said coldly. Anger and the desire to run suffused her every fiber. "Then forget it!" Janna said even more coldly.

David looked into her eyes. She had no idea what he saw. She really DIDN'T know him. "His letter was right," she thought.

"In thirty minutes," David said.

They agreed to meet on the beach.

Janna almost hated herself for going. She thought of leaving the island instead. "Surprise him—just GO," she thought.

She was waiting when he arrived at the meeting place on the beach.

They talked. The girl was still there. Yes, they were sleeping together.

"Where'd she come from?" Janna asked.

Some friend of his had dropped her off. She would be leaving in a couple of days.

"Send her NOW," Janna said desperately.

Janna and David looked into each other's eyes. They drew near and kissed.

Janna could hear herself moaning. She was lost. She let go and drowned in love for David.

They drew back and looked at each other. Janna trembled inside.

"You'll just have to trust me on this one," David said.

"Okay," Janna said, "but this is the LAST one."

"Trust me," David said again and Janna did.

She felt sick watching him drive away. She belonged to him—she and she alone.

The night was a torture for Janna. She longed for his arms and lay in bed with a leaden heart. She felt so lost, so lonely. Tears saturated her face and hair. At last she slept, her face pressed into a dampened pillow.

No ghostly lovers came. No one came to ease her pain.

\*

The next day Janna spoke to herself about self-esteem and pride. She almost persuaded herself to leave—to go forever for she knew she couldn't live under the conditions she'd found herself involved in. South of France looked almost good. She was tempted to rebound there. She could handle France now. Nothing there could touch the ice she felt in her heart.

The memory of David's kiss was frightening. She wanted to run from it.

Janna wanted David. She wanted him and she knew it. She HAD to admit it.

She found herself, again, contriving to see him. He was at the 'Watering Hole' when she drove by. She pulled over and he came to her car.

She heard herself asking him to go on a short trip with her. She heard herself BEG.

David said, "I'll try."

"It would make things better," she thought. It could help right some of the wrong of the girl if he'd leave her to go with Janna, leaving the girl behind. Pride asked Janna why it had been sacrificed to the folly of a fool. She had no answers to appease it.

*

Janna tried to write the next day but the words wouldn't come. She finally decided to go to the village.

As she pulled up to the 'Watering Hole' and saw David going across the street to the bar and grill. His truck was parked there and Wad stood beside it.

David saw her and came over to talk to her. She had a gut feeling he'd changed his mind. She sat in her car as he came over.

The island was overflowing with tourists. It seemed to be some sort of holiday. Janna remembered posters as she'd come through the small town on the mainland and stopped for gas that there was a seafood festival or something going on.

David and Wad crossed the street. She watched his face as he came toward her. She knew he wasn't going to follow the suggestion he had made in the letter and get away for a couple of days with her to get better acquainted. Janna was hurt and angry at being let down. She had hoped they could go to

Tallahassee for a day or two for she'd never been there but had seen pictures of the beautiful capital city of Florida.

David's eyes met hers. "You aren't going, are you?" she asked. Her heart was sick. Now she knew she'd not return to the island and would definitely leave the next day. She would go to Tallahassee and she'd go alone and after that she'd decide.

David swore he had to work and couldn't get away. There was a deadline and the builder was pushing him. He looked genuinely sorry but she was unhappy with his decision.

"None of this is working out," Janna said. "I will be going to Tallahassee tomorrow."

"What's in Tallahassee?" he asked. "<u>You</u> could have been," she said. "I've never been there and there's some shopping I want to do."

David turned suddenly and shouted to Wad, "GET OUT OF THE STREET!" He scolded him and Wad looked crestfallen. He hid behind Janna's car. David turned to speak to her and spun back around.

A car flashed by. It held a bunch of yelling laughing teens.

Wad jumped toward the road. He was probably going to sit and sulk beside his beloved truck.

Janna saw the car, saw Wad and grayed out. She staggered from her car to stand beside David.

The teenagers stopped. They weren't laughing any longer.

David said nothing could be done.

Janna begged for a vet but David knew Wad was dying.

Janna knelt to hold Wad's paw. Her heart broke to watch him die. She knew what he meant to David and she liked him herself. She thought of her little dogs and knew how lost she'd be without them. Her heart was bleak with misery.

David walked to sit on a nearby bench. Wad had been his best friend. Janna thought, "Now I've caused him to lose Wad."

Wad lay lifeless and she felt David had withdrawn from her for forever. She looked down at Wad. "We've both lost our lives," she thought.

People came by to hug David. He waved them aside. She sat on the bench beside him and cried silently and so did he.

David got up at last and walked over to Wad. He picked him up and placed him on the bed of his truck.

David's grief was great. Janna was horrified to see him strike Wad's lifeless body. "I WARNED you to stay out of the street! I told you a million times!" he shouted.

Janna caught his arm. He looked at her. "He would have learned," he said. "He was young; he just didn't have the time."

David cursed the tourists who were so careless. This wasn't the first animal he'd lost but it was his dearest.

He went to open the truck door. Janna asked if he wanted her to come along.

"No, I'll see you later," David said. He drove away with Wad.

Janna turned and ran. She cried for Wad. She cried for David and she cried for herself.

As she ran, she saw David's truck on the street parallel to hers. They ran along side by side for awhile and as the truck gained speed it pulled ahead. She could see Wad lying in the truck bed where he once stood so proudly. Her grief was limitless and she knew

David was inconsolable. Janna turned back to walk slowly back to her car. She was dripping with sweat from her running. "That's all I do," she thought. "RUN, RUN, RUN."

Janna went home. The house welcomed her. She lay on her daybed and cried herself dry. Her little dogs cuddled her close. She fell asleep and slept the sleep of the exhausted.

When she woke up it was quiet and dark. She looked at her watch and found it was earlier than she expected.

She let the dogs out for awhile as she showered and put on fresh shorts and a shirt.

She let the dogs in and played with them for awhile.

She was restless. She knew writing was out of the question. She wandered around the house downstairs. She never went upstairs. Finally, she got her purse and keys and went to the village.

She didn't stop at the 'Watering Hole' for she knew she couldn't handle any further trauma. She went, instead to the place where she'd had margaritas with Hoyt and Joan. The place was crowded. The tourists were out in droves and the band played loud amid the laughter and talk.

Janna saw Hoyt and he waved her over. Janna caught her breath as she saw David walk over toward Hoyt's table at the same time.

She looked at Hoyt and he said, "I forced him to come out." People walked past David and clapped him on the shoulder or hugged him. It was like a wake.

Janna walked to his side and slipped her arm around his waist. He turned toward her and they held each other. He said quietly, "The girl left the next day. I meant to tell you but—."

Janna said, "It's past."

He looked at her and answered, "Yes, it is."

Several people looked toward them. "I'm getting drunk tonight," David said. "Will you see that I get home?"

Janna's soft heart had forgiven him. She said, "Yes, I will watch after you." Her love still burned beneath the sadness.

Many people hugged David, often without words.

David drank several mixed drinks. She had never seen him drink anything but beer. He asked her to dance and they danced. Janna knew she'd be taking David home that night. She'd hold him in her arms all night. And she'd be there for him in his time of need. The other girl was gone but she, Janna, was there to stay. "Janna and David—forever," she thought and her sadness rested.

"Are you ready to go?" David finally asked.

"Yes," Janna answered. She held his arm as he stumbled on their way to her car.

They lay together that night at David's place. The narrow bed held them with room to spare. There was no question of sex. Comforting was what David needed and holding him in her arms brought her peace.

Their bodies intertwined and the next morning they still lay as they'd fallen asleep. Janna and David together at last.

*

Janna stayed home by day and with David at night.

They spoke of sex after a few days.

"I'll be faithful," David said, "but do you think it's fair to say 'no sex' unless there's marriage? We need time to know each other."

The same old song and dance, Janna thought. Why don't men EVER learn? "NO SEX," she repeated.

Janna, herself, wondered how they'd resolve sleeping together without sex. She wondered how difficult it would be for David to remain faithful under those conditions. She knew if he were ever unfaithful, ever had another girl after they were together, that she would never see him again. She had never been in such a dilemma. She didn't want to become one of David's love 'em and leave 'em women. She had to be honest with herself. Neither of them were ready to just dash off to the alter.

Janna had been 'shell shocked' as she called it after the south of France. Someone who had charmed her so completely had not been the person she thought he was at all. The relationship had started easy and ended so cruelly. There hadn't been enough space between then and now.

David said he thought he loved her. He'd tell her when he was sure. She smiled at his audacity. She thought she could bring him to his sorrow for being such an idiot. She could leave. In her woman's wisdom she saw his fear. He was afraid he couldn't hold her. He didn't want to invest himself completely. He didn't realize he already had. It was written in the stars. Deep inside Janna knew.

Janna smiled at David. "I have set a date in my mind. When that date comes and we are no closer than we are now, I'll leave."

David tried to find out the date. "He's such a CHILD and so much a MAN," she thought of the contradiction.

The date was her birthday—in January.

The date in her mind had been a real decision. If by her birthday he wasn't sure enough to ask for marriage then she was leaving. Janna wasn't the type to travel down a one way street forever. She knew the deadline—he didn't.

She decided to love him until then. Love him as though it were to be forever, to love him passionately.

That night they made love. They were both afraid, wanting so desperately to please each other.

Janna was happy that night and all the nights they loved.

David held back the words, "I love you."

Something cold and hurting smiled sadly in the bottom of Janna's heart. A shadow would cross her eyes. She knew she'd go on her birthday, then David spoke the tender words of love.

Janna felt the hurt dissolve. She couldn't touch him enough, look at him enough, or kiss him enough.

David seemed to feel much the same.

Once the mutual love was settled, they became a couple around the island.

David was still elusive as to the question of marriage.

Janna knew the deadline. She smiled sadly to herself. "Play all you like," she thought, "for when my birthday comes, I'll disappear from this island and never return, no matter what. I won't be a party to my own heartache." Her decision was written in stone, the cold stone of her wounded heart.

\*

One night David and Janna sat at a local place on the bay. Tall frozen margaritas were placed before them.

David raised his glass. "I love you," he said. "I love you so much."

Janna looked into his beautiful eyes.

"I'm going to propose to you," he said.

Janna was shocked. She wanted it but hadn't expected it. "Be still my heart!" she said a little wryly.

"I'm ASKING you to marry me," David said. "Janna, will you marry me?"

Janna's heart emptied pain, her world filled and overfilled with joy. "Yes," she answered simply. "Yes, David."

David made the announcement immediately and several friends crowded around to congratulate them. Everyone was happy for them and a little surprised.

Lovemaking that night had a special meaning for Janna. It felt right. She was no prude and she was no virgin. She just wanted a pure and permanent relationship with the man—the only man—she had truly ever loved.

Sex had been good for them. Now it was glorious.

They slept tenderly and beautifully together that night. The next night they moved in together at the Diehl house. They would have a month and a half before anyone was scheduled to come on the time-share. Janna wanted the time to be spent in the home she loved, with the man she loved. She wanted to love him on her family bed and in the room that had affected her so strongly. She had avoided the room, but it had never been far from her mind. She was drawn to it and yet was afraid to go into it alone. Now she was obsessed with the desire to sleep in the room with David.

That night she led David to the room. The large brass bed gleamed in the soft light.

The crotchet spread was a field of paleness that beckoned to them.

Several generations of Janna's family had slept in the bed before it had been taken to the attic because someone hadn't wanted to keep the beautiful brass polished.

Janna stood beside the bed. "This is a special bed," she told David. "Both of my grandparents died on this bed. People in my family slept in this bed on their wedding nights. They gave birth on this bed and they died on this bed. I want to sleep here with you. When my sister and I were small and if there was a storm we'd jump into the middle of this bed and feel safe."

Janna and David made love on the bed, adding to its special history. Janna dreamed of twins. Their names were Janis and David.

David had to work the next day. She felt him slip from the bed early that morning leaving a kiss on her forehead before he left the room. She felt differently about being in the room alone. She was happy and she belonged in this room with David.

The early morning sun tipped into the window some time after she heard David's big truck roar to a start and pull away. The sun caught the posts of the bed turning them into gleaming gold. The bay sparkled in the distance outside the window.

Janna got up and stood in the window. She felt closed in and opened it wide. The hillside caught her attention. A large solid white bird stood on the gray stone. As she watched, another one joined it. They placed their beaks together. Janna smiled.

Janna walked to the bed and straightened it lovingly. As she went downstairs, she paused a moment beside the carving on the banister. She remembered her dream of the twins.

*

David had left her some crisp fried bacon. She toasted some bread and poached an egg. Coffee was made and waiting. "I could get used to this," she said aloud.

She took her second cup of coffee out to the sun porch. Her little dogs wanted out. She had heard David let them out earlier. She'd laughed as he whistled and called for them. He had called out, "Come here, what's your names!"

Janna sipped her coffee and hummed happily at some half-remembered melody.

She took the cup to the kitchen and rinsed it out on her way to the bath. She could smell the scent of last night's lovemaking on her body. She felt light and dreamy still.

During her bath, Janna's thoughts turned to her book. She had put it aside too many times. She was ready to write again. She couldn't wait to get dressed. Ideas were fighting for space in her head. She didn't want to forget anything.

She hurried out to the porch in her robe and began to write notes furiously. Finally she came to a stopping place and went back to finish getting dressed for the day.

She went outside after she was dressed. Her little dogs were spoiling for attention. She took them to the beach and watched them chase birds and dodge waves. She ran with them, feeling she'd never been happier in her life.

The sky was a cloudless blue; the water was bathed in sunlight that highlighted the frothy tips of the lively waves. Aquas and blues mingled in an ecstasy of colors. Pelicans flew over in formation and a ship bound for some unknown location seemed to move slowly across the horizon.

The gulf breeze teased Janna's long hair. She kicked off her shoes and ran into the gulf. Muffy and Puffy barked for her to come back to the beach as she dove into a big wave.

The water was warm with little cool currents. Janna swam and played with a heart so full of joy it seemed to overflow.

Muffy and Puffy couldn't stand watching her play in the water without them. They finally joined her. Their fluffy hair collapsed, as they became soaked in the water. They looked like little seals as they dog paddled beside her.

Janna walked to shore and they followed, shaking sprays of water all over her as they tried to shake themselves dry.

When they got back to the house, Janna filled the bathtub and prepared to wash the dogs. It was strange how they always seemed to know when they were to be bathed. They both were hiding when Janna called for them.

Janna laughed as she spotted Muffy's tail sticking out from under her daybed. She looked under the bed and found Puffy hiding there also. She dragged them out by force one by one as it was their turn. Next she had to shampoo her hair and start all over getting herself dressed.

Janna made a quick sandwich and took it and a glass of milk along to the sun porch. Her mind worked on her book as she ate.

After lunch she wrote again. The words and ideas came rapidly, the story flowed out in wild jubilation. It had been bottled up for

too long.   "This will be my best book yet,"
Janna thought.

As the day grew late, Janna watched eagerly
for David's return.   It seemed an eternity
before the big truck lumbered up to the
driveway.

David got out and walked up the steps.
Janna stood on the porch.   Her eyes sparkled
with love.   She reached up to kiss him.

"I'm dirty," he said.

"Doesn't matter," Janna said and their arms
went around each other.   His faint manly odor
excited her.   She'd never felt such a sense of
'wifehood'.

Janna's life had not been like those of her
old school chums from Iowa.   She'd not been
able to sit home and wait eagerly for the man
of her dreams to come home after work.   Janna
was delighted as they walked inside arm in
arm.

David showered, then he and Janna sat on the
back porch sipping cold beers.   He spoke of
his day at work and Janna showed him what she
had written.   They delighted in each other's
talents.   He was building a house and she was
building a book.

"If I died now," Janna thought, "I'd be
leaving this earth happier than I've ever been
in my life."

The sweetness of the evening was complete
when David told her he had told probably about
thirty people about their engagement.

They spent the evening after a simple meal
reading and talking, often kissing, hugging
and looking into each other's eyes.   The night
was perfect.   Janna decided to share her
secrets of the house with David.

"David," she said, "I want to tell you
something—but I don't want you to laugh at me

or think what I'm about to say is just plain crazy, okay?"

"Well, tell me first," David said, ruffling her hair, "and then we'll see. I already know you're crazy or you wouldn't be marrying such a clod as me."

"Well, I love this clod," Janna said running her hand over his body, moving to touch in a special place.

David kissed her. "So tell me," he prompted.

She told him about the room that Janie and Jake had shared—the one where they'd spent the night before with such closeness. She told him of the experience she'd had the first and only time she had been in the room before he and she had slept in it the night before. She spoke of how it seemed to beckon her when they were to at last spend the night there in the house. She spoke of the sadness she felt as she touched the names carved on the banister and about the cold air that had slid past her as she paused beside the names. He laughed when she spoke of the dream lover and kissed her when she told him she honestly believed it was his spirit that had come to comfort and love her. She paused waiting for David's reaction.

David had listened intently. He told her of his own fascinated with house, it had been a lifetime fascination. He told her how he got the chills and the hair on his arms stood up when he came near the house. He related to her the story that he might be somehow related to the people who had built the house. Their names had been the same as his, for his male ancestors had brought the name down from somewhere. He thought the abandoned baby had been given that last name but had no idea as

to why. The Indian family who raised the
child certainly wouldn't have been named
Diehl.

"Speaking of the room," David teased her,
"why don't we go try it out?" He kissed her
and they both ran up the stairs. Janna's hand
felt the indentation on the banister and she
hurried past, her hand trailing behind.

David stopped almost toppling her over.
"Wait," he said. "I want to see those names."

David peered closely. "Janna and David?" he
asked.

"No, Janis and David, it reads. Some other
lovers from the past."

"I still think it's us," David said and held
her close. He suddenly tightened his arms
around her body. "We must never lose each
other," he whispered huskily.

Janna's eyes swam in tears of tenderness.
"Never," she answered quietly and they were
both startled by the current of cold air that
brushed their shoulders like a passing caress.

"There it is again!" David said, "Did you
feel it too?"

"Yes," she answered, her eyes wide with
wonder.

They walked toward the room, their arms
around each other.

Janna hung back as David opened the door.
The light from the hallway sent a soft weak
light into the room. The patterns of light
and shadow seemed to swirl.

"Strange," David said, reaching for the
light switch.

"I'm sorry," he apologized as the light
switched on.

"For what?" Janna asked.

"I didn't know you were turning on the
light, too," he said.

Janna looked at him. "I WASN'T," she said, "You turned it on!"

David cupped her chin and laughed as he kissed her. "I'd know your soft, sweet hand anywhere," he said.

"David, I really wasn't turning on the light and you know it. I knew you would tease me!"

David looked serious. "You're putting ME on," he said. "Be honest, I started to turn on the light and my hand touched someone else's hand—they flicked the switch—not me. You did it, you little tease, so admit it!" He grabbed her and started to tickle her ribs, which he knew she couldn't bear.

"No! No! Please don't! I hate that!" she gasped struggling to get free.

"Okay," David said, "IF you tell the truth." He was laughing.

Janna felt tears gather in her eyes. One slid down her cheek as she shook her head. "I really didn't, Honey," she said quietly.

David reached out to hold her. "Are you afraid?" he asked.

"I don't know WHAT I am," Janna said, her teary eyes wide with wonder. "I don't think I'm so much afraid as I am shocked."

"Do you want to sleep in here again tonight?" David asked.

"Last night was beautiful," Janna said. "Tonight I'm just a little spooked." She glanced out the window. Shadows seemed to move on the hillside.

They left, closing the door behind them. Neither of them wanted to sleep upstairs in any of the bedrooms that night. They slept on the daybed on the back porch. David held her close and Janna cuddled into the curve of his body. She smiled when she felt the two little dogs hop up to find some space at their feet.

Janna felt cozy and safe. She was at home, no matter what was going on upstairs.

*

"Will you be okay here today?" David asked the next morning as he left for work.

"Yes, the days are so peaceful here," Janna answered.

"Want to stay at my house tonight?" he asked.

"Yes," Janna replied, "but when we come back here, we'll sleep in that room again. "There's something in that room that draws me but I can't stand being in it alone. I think that since I first saw it I've had a longing to sleep there with my love. At that time I had no love. The night we slept there was wonderful but I did have a dream. The dream was about twin babies named Janis and David. No doubt the carving on the banister brought that on. It was strange though: I thought I was their mother."

"Whoa!" David laughed. "Twins!"

"I'm not sure I can even get pregnant," Janna said.

"I don't think I can get anyone pregnant, either," David admitted. "I've never got anyone pregnant yet."

Janna looked at him and shook her head. "Well, let's don't get into that!" she said.

"We could sleep there tonight," David said. "If you do want to sleep there with your love."

"Let's wait awhile," Janna said. She walked him to the door and kissed him goodbye.

Janna stood on the porch watching his big truck drive away. The little dogs played outside. She sat on the steps and watched

116

them.  All of the mingled island scents lay in the soft breeze.  She was so happy, so at home.

She sat on the steps daydreaming of David. She loved him beyond everything.  She thought of how he had stepped from the gulf in the moonlight.  "It was a symbolic birth," she thought.  "He was born for me and I was born for him."

Janna went inside and wrote until lunch. She ate a salad and drank some apple juice. She went back to her book then stood up and walked out the back door.  The gray stones had puzzled her from the time she'd first seen them.  She remembered the shadowy movements she'd seen hovering over the stones the night before.  She thought of the story of the unmarked graves that Flonzie and natives of the island had spoken of.  It was probably a reflection she'd seen off the stones last night, she thought, but she wanted to see them up close.

The way to the hillside was more tangled in vines and undergrowth than she'd realized.

Once determined to see the hillside and the gray stones she struggled on.

She was perspiring and had been scratched and snagged as she worked her way up the hill.

"I feel like I've climbed Mt. Everest!" she laughed at herself, as she mopped sweat from her face with her shirttail.

She stopped to examine the stone at her feet.  It had obviously been cut to a specific size.  It had fallen over and several small pieces lay near by.

Janna could see the other large stone had been less damaged.  It lay a few feet from the other one.  Janna climbed over large vines and knelt to turn it over to see if it had an inscription on the underside. It was some sort of a tombstone, she was sure. There were no inscriptions on either stone or on any of the scattered pieces of the first one. "That's odd," she thought and began to gather the broken pieces to lay beside the stone they had been broken off of. Thick vines grew tightly around one of the larger pieces. She tugged determinedly to slide it from underneath their grasp. She finally freed the stone and found no inscription on it either. She moved to place it near the corner it had been broken off of. She stepped forward and bent to place the stone against the other one. Suddenly the footing that had appeared to be solid gave away and she felt herself plunge downward through a net of vines and leaves.

Her foot broke through rotting timbers and a sharp twig scraped her right side as she fell. She thought she might be bleeding from the wound. "Oh! No!" she moaned as she tried to free her feet. She struggled to bring up her knees as she held onto a thick vine.

She panicked as she fought the ensnaring tangle of vine and roots only to fall deeper and be held tighter in the surrounding roots growing deep into the pit.

She thought she'd fallen through some sort of old wooden platform. She was terrified that she was suspended above an old abandoned well. Her eyes were barely level with the rim of the pit. She could see down the hillside through some of the underbrush. Even if she called out there was no one to hear her. The dogs were inside the house. David was at work.

Janna moved cautiously. One of her arms hooked over a thick vine. The rest of her body seemed to be surrounded by less

substantial growth. Her feet dangled, trapped
in a hole with no bottom that she could reach
by turning her toes downward seeking something
below. The thought of being suspended above a
bottomless pit was terrifying. The thought
that it might be filled with water, and
probably was, due to the water table of the
island, almost caused her to faint from fear.

She thought of David and hung on. She
thought of Janie, Jake and the kids. She had
to live.

The Florida sun beat down unmercifully. Her
arm began to tingle, as her circulation was
restricted. She wiggled her fingers
frantically. The arm became dead and heavy.
She knew she had to change her position or
she'd soon fall.

She reached across her body slowly, caught
the thick vine with her other hand and worked
the deadened arm into a better position. She
found she couldn't hold on that way for it
twisted her body painfully. Her side hurt and
her back felt like it would break from the
pressure.

Grasping the vine tightly, she used her arm
to help dislodge her deadened arm. It fell
beside her almost useless but beginning to
tingle painfully as the blood began to move
along the vessels again.

She worked her body into a more bearable
position. She moved slowly, careful as she
worked the vine into the crook of her arm,
letting her fingers travel up the convoluted
trunk to hold on, to have better support for
her dangling body.

As she grasped the vine with her fingers,
the skin on the trunk slipped and she sank a
few inches further down in the hole.

The view of the hillside vanished from her sight. Now she saw only dirt, vines, and dried vegetation that had fallen into the hole over a period of many years.

A blazing sun glared above her head. Her feet were suspended above she knew not what. Her imagination was loose with horrible possibilities.

Something rustled in the underbrush.

Janna's hopes surged. "David!" she screamed.

The rustling stopped.

"David! David! David!" she shrieked.

No one answered.

"Help! Anyone!" she screamed.

The rustling went away down the hillside. She thought of alligators. "Oh! God! Please help me," she prayed and began to cry. Her mind wouldn't be calm. She thought, what if that was a snake? If anything crawled on her she would be helpless.

Her eyes fastened on the top of the hole. She saw a spider crawl down the vine. It paused before crawling over her arm.

Janna was mute with horror. The spider continued downward. "How many more are down there?" Janna wondered and felt her skin crawl.

Something else moved along the leaves and dirt under the rim of the pit. Janna's eyes were huge as she watched a slender, gleaming body reveal a portion of itself, then slither deeper into the stench of rotting loam.

The movement drew closer to her face. "Oh, God!" she moaned, imagining a snakebite to her face.

She screamed as the lizard popped its head out inches before her eyes. They stared at each other in horror. She heard herself

shrieking.     She  held  the  vine  desperately.
When  she  opened  her  eyes  the  lizard  was  gone.
Sweat  and  tears  blurred  her  vision  of  the
tangled  mess  before  her  eyes.

She  was  afraid  to  move  the  hand  that  was
still  tingling  itself  awake  to  wipe  her  face.
Salty  sweat  and  tears  ran  into  her  mouth.

Janna  was  immobilized  with  terror  and  the
necessity  to  hang  on  to  the  vine.     She  was
thirsty  and  the  sun  showed  no  remorse.

Eternity  seemed  to  stretch  before  her  as  the
day  wore  on  slowly.     She  resolved  to  think
only  of  David.     Her  mind  called  out  to  him.

The  sun  moved  down  the  hillside  leaving
shadows  in  place  of  it's  piercing  rays.     "How
much  longer?"  she  wondered.     Her  arm  hurt  and
her  shoulder  ached  from  the  stress  it  was
enduring.     She  tried  to  move  her  limbs
carefully  to  keep  circulation  in  them.

She  clung  desperately  to  the  thick  vine.
She  felt  as  though  it  had  embedded  itself  into
her  flesh.

The  sky  above  darkened  and  the  pit  became
dim.     Birds  called  to  each  other  and  things
above  and  below  her  continued  to  rustle.     She
listened  anxiously  for  the  sound  of  the  big
truck.

Mosquitoes  came  with  dusk.     Janna  cried
helplessly  as  they  drove  themselves  into  her
body  and  sucked  their  painful  fill  of  her
blood.     Each  bite  was  added  agony.

Janna  felt  faint.     Blackness  deepened  in  the
world  around  her  and  in  her  mind.     She  felt
her  arm  slipping  as  the  muscles  fell  slack
from  continuing  stress.     She  couldn't  hold  on.

Suddenly  adrenaline  gushed  to  her  heart.     A
man's  figure  stood  at  the  side  of  the  pit.     A
woman's  figure  rose  to  stand  beside  him.     They
leaned  toward  her.     "Please  wait  for  David,"

they seemed to say. Their eyes held love for her. "Please wait for David," they begged.

Reality had lost meaning for Janna. They were her reality. They were with her in her desperation. She had new strength. The adrenaline had renewed the muscles in her arm. She would wait for David.

Janna held her arm crooked into the vine. She shuddered at how close she'd been to falling into the horror below.

Janna raised her shoulder and bunched the muscles. It hurt like hell. She looked up to find the comfort of the shadowy figures above her. They were gone.

A truck ground to a stop down the hillside. A door slammed and Janna screamed for David.

There was no answer.

She heard the door to the house close. Her dogs were barking. She could tell they were outside. She continued to scream.

She heard David come outside and call to the dogs.

She screamed again. Her throat was raw.

"Janna?" David called back.

She began to cry.

"Janna?" he called again.

Screams tore from her throat. She heard a crackling in the underbrush as he worked his way toward her.

"Be careful!" she called out. "I'm in a deep hole. I think it's a well!"

"I hear you, Honey!" he called to her still some distance away. "Just hang in there, I'm coming!"

"The words 'hang in there' brought her to hysteria. She felt wild laughter escape her lips. She fought to control it. "I'm in a HOLE!" she called to him again. "It's by the stones! Be careful!"

She heard him fighting to get through the vines. Soon he stood above her. He reached down to pull her up. Her legs were trapped.

"If you pull on me you'll break my legs," Janna cried. "I don't know how we'll get me out! I'm hung up down there somehow." David lay on his stomach holding her under her arms. He couldn't pull her free and it was hurting her too much trying to do it that way. He spoke words of comfort, of reassurance, of love.

"Could you hold on to that vine again for a little while longer?" David asked. "I need to get a light and a few things from the truck." He leaned down to kiss her lips.

"Yes, but hurry," she said needlessly. She crooked her arm into the vine. David was there and she knew he'd get her free. She heard him crashing back down the hill.

Her two little dogs had worked themselves up the hillside and they whined as they hung their little faces over the edge of the hole. She could see their fuzzy outlines against the pale moonlight. She talked to them. Muffy let out a piteous little howl. "It's okay, Sweetie," she comforted her. "David is going to rescue me." She talked to Muffy and Puffy until David came crashing back up the hill.

His arms were loaded with items for Janna's rescue. The big flashlight bobbed around throwing light onto his face, the dogs, and in Janna's eyes.

Janna heard his breath coming in gasps and she knew he'd run through the undergrowth, probably falling as he did so.

David soon had a thick rope about Janna's shoulders. It rested beneath each armpit. It was looped around her snugly and tied to a tree. She couldn't slide down any further.

She heaved a sigh of relief. The pain was excruciating but she was glad to be secured. She had feared falling into the pit all the while she'd been in the hole. She was safe from whatever lurked below. "This won't feel good, Honey, but it will hold you up until I can cut loose whatever is holding you below."

Janna was afraid David would, also, fall into the pit.

"No," he said. "I made a loop in the other end of the rope and I have that around me."

He lowered himself down beside her. The beam of the flashlight thrust illumination into the pit. Janna closed her eyes against it's glare. She felt David kiss her softly as he worked his body downward past her. The bright light followed him down. She could hear and feel him cutting away roots and vines.

Finally her feet were free. "You're not over a well," he told her.

"What was it?" she rasped out from a swollen throat.

"I'll tell you later," he said. She thought she heard him chuckle. "What's this?" she heard him say to himself.

"What's WHAT?" she asked in a croak.

"Buried treasure, maybe," he said, "or at least an old metal box."

"Can you get it up?" she asked, every word grating into the soreness of her throat.

"Tomorrow," David said, working his way back up the rope. "Tonight, YOU—tomorrow, the box." He worked his way past Janna and over the edge of the pit.

He leaned over and caught her under her arms. She heard him grunt with exertion as he pulled her upward. As her torso emerged she grabbed him around the waist.

He lifted her to stand beside him. Her legs were like rubber. She couldn't stand.

David lifted her to his back and carried her piggy back down the hillside.

She heard him breathing heavily as he carefully planted his feet among the heavy vegetation.

The little dogs leaped around trying to overcome the ensnaring.

Janna hurt everywhere, she even seemed to feel each and every mosquito bite. Her side felt gummy and she knew it was drying blood. She clung to David.

David placed Janna on the daybed. He stripped off her filthy, bloodstained clothing and bathed her body in lukewarm water. Then he came back in with a soothing antiseptic for the mosquito bites. He carefully washed the open wounds with warm soapy water and rinsed them in clean warm water. He spread some medication that burned somewhat over the wounds and dressed them with gauze over the salve.

"Your face is very sunburned, Honey," he said as he gently massaged cream over her hot red face.

Janna surrendered to David. He would make her well. Exhaustion swept over her in waves. She wavered in and out of sleep. The pain medication that David had found in the medicine cabinet helped somewhat. It was an over the counter medicine and wasn't very strong.

At one point Janna opened her eyes to see that David had removed his clothing. She saw his beautiful naked body in the moonlight as she had seen it that night on the beach.

As David carefully lowered his body to the bed to lie next to her she saw the man and

125

woman in the doorway. They stood hand in hand watching her and David.

Her hand reached for the sheet to cover her naked body; she paused and let it drop for she knew it didn't matter. The grayness of fatigue claimed her and she slept.

Her next memory was of David trying to ease from the bed without waking her.

It was morning. She put out her hand and touched his naked back.

He turned to kiss her softly. "Sleep, Janna," he said. "I'm not working today. I'll be here with you."

She was sore all over. She groaned and closed her eyes. She soon slept, sometimes breaking through to a twilight sleep to hear a rustle of pages being turned in a book or a slight cough. She knew David watched over her and she fell into a deep, dreamless peacefulness.

When she finally woke it was three o'clock in the afternoon. She was starving, thirsty and ached everywhere.

David helped her up, her muscles screamed at the abuse. She went to the bathroom. She was shocked at her injuries. A rough red scrape around a gouge ran down her side. Blood and a scab crusted its edge. Other smaller cuts and scrapes were here and there and several bruises were beginning to turn colors. She groaned at her sunburned face, which was red, blotched and puffy. Cold water and make-up didn't help a lot. "Vanity," she thought.

She returned to the smell of bacon. David was fixing bacon and eggs. He handed her a cup of coffee.

"Could I help?" she asked.

He looked at her and shook his head. He pulled out a chair. "Sit," he said, going back to the stove.

Janna held the table and painfully lowered herself into the chair. David walked over with a plate of food. "Want me to feed you?" he asked, touching her reddened cheek with his hand.

"Of course not!" she laughed. Her face stretched painfully.

"I know it hurts," he said. "Now eat. We'll talk later." He brought a cold glass of juice from the refrigerator. She gulped it down. It felt wonderful to her feverish throat. She thought of the metal box David had found.

"Did pirates ever live on this island?" she asked.

"Yes," David answered, "now sh-s-s-sh! Eat first!"

Janna ate quickly. David took her plate to the sink.

"What was in the box?" she asked.

"Let's get you settled back in bed and I'll tell you," he said.

He helped her to bed and returned to bring her a glass of cold water and a couple of aspirin. "You're feverish," he said.

"THE BOX?" Janna insisted, her curiosity was eating her up.

David laughed. "First of all, you didn't fall into a old well, but into what appears to be an old grave."

Janna was horrified. She listened intently remembering now the story old Flonzie had told of the graves that had been found on the property.

"The island is sand for the most part, and the grave collapsed eventually and the sand was gradually washed out as it flooded from time to time, is my guess. Old and new vegetation filled the cavern, their roots loosening the sand further as they nosed their way downward. What you thought was an old wooden platform was the remains of an old coffin—probably cypress and homemade."

"Oh! No!" Janna shuddered. "My feet were trapped in a COFFIN? How horrible! I would have died of a heart attack if I'd known! Thinking it was a well was bad enough!" She sank back into her pile of pillows.

"I think it definitely was a coffin," David said.

Janna told David of the trip she and Janie had made to the nursing home. She told him of Flonzie's story of the two graves with no inscriptions.

"Then I would say there were two graves there," David said. "I believe they caved in together and merged due to the years of erosion and plant invasion. The hole is like a small cave up under those roots and vines."

Janna told him of the man and woman who came to her as she gave up trying to hold on there in the pit. She told him she KNEW they were pleading for her to wait for him, and then she remembered how they'd stood in the doorway hand in hand, to see her and David to bed.

David didn't laugh at her. "Janis and David—forever," he said softly. "I wish we could KNOW."

"NOW," Janna said, "what about the box?"

"I don't know," David answered, "I haven't been back up there. I wanted to talk to you first and, also, I wanted to be nearby when you woke up. You went through HELL. I can only imagine what it was like, and what I imagine you went through is pretty awful.

Then, too, Janna, this property, whatever it is, belongs to your family and there is a question of whether it would be right to remove the box from the grave. Grave robbing, you know?"

Janna smiled stiffly at David. She loved his logic and honesty. In fact, she loved everything about him. "The graves are unmarked, maybe something there will give us a clue as to the occupant's identity. Maybe the ghosts of this house want to be known, at last," she said.

David kissed her. "Do you want me to get it?" he asked.

"I'll help," Janna said and groaned as she tried to rise.

"Janna, you stay HERE," David said. "It wasn't that easy carrying you off that hillside last night, and you, my love, aren't up to the walk. You just rest here and I'll be back before long."

The little dogs tried to follow him out the door. "You little balls of fluff, stay here, too," he ordered, shutting the door in their disappointed little faces.

Janna lay propped on her pillows. She could see him as he worked his way up to the hillside. A rope was coiled and slung over his shoulder. When he reached the crest of the hill the dark foliage of vines and twisted trees silhouetted him. She saw him stoop to examine the stones then take the rope from his shoulder. He worked with the rope for awhile then bent over and disappeared from sight.

Janna was terrified for him as she remembered how she'd felt trapped in the hole.

A door upstairs slammed and Janna felt sweat pop out on the tight, dry skin of her face. She wondered if David had been upstairs looking for her last night before he'd found her outside. Maybe he had left a door open and some draft had slammed it shut. Somehow she didn't think that was it.

Footsteps seemed to whisper on the stairs and a door slammed again. "David?" Janna called and no one answered. The hackles rose on the back of her neck. The cold chills that ran over her body may have been due to her feverish condition, but she doubted it. She watched desperately for David.

A soft glow seemed to hover over the place where David had disappeared. Janna grew anxious.

It seemed an eternity before David reappeared. Janna had called her little dogs to cuddle up beside her. She could see he carried something in his hand. He sat it down and coiled his rope back up. He held the object in his hand as he stood looking down into the graves.

Janna loved him so dearly as she watched him make the sign of the cross over the graves.

He put the coiled rope over his shoulder and Janna watched as he struggled through the vines and tangled vegetation. She thought of how hard it must have been for him to carry her over that jungle of growth and not to stumble in the process.

It was with a sigh of relief that she saw him appear at the sun porch door.

He stopped to drop the rope and remove his boots.

When he stepped inside he held a large rusted box in his hands. He lay it on the table beside Janna's bed.

Thick rusted iron bands held the box together. A chunk of rust covered the place where a keyhole had probably been.

"I'll have to chip some of this away," David said.

He left the room to return with a newspaper, chisel and few other tools. The box was reluctant to open.

Janna watched with anticipation.

At last David pried off the lid to the box.

Janna leaned forward as David lifted out an old leather covered book. A metal cover was over the leather-bound book. The metal was pierced into a lacey filigree. A cross and some stones clung to the front of the book. Some rust and tarnish had found their way inside the metal box and marred the beauty of the metal. Mother of pearl still gleamed among the stones set into the cross. It had been a beautiful volume. David laid it carefully on the newspaper.

A few trinkets were tucked around the book. David lifted them out carefully. There was a babies ring of gold, a tiny locket, a little spoon, very tarnished as the cross was and probably silver; a roll of fabric that was fragile and falling apart. It had been a beautiful long lace baby dress with matching bonnet. It had been satin and lace. The lace was beautiful and had overlaid the satin backing. "It's probably a christening outfit," Janna said. "A baby must have been buried there."

"Maybe a still born and not yet named," David said. "That could explain the lack of inscriptions on the stone."

"STONES," Janna reminded him "Could have the weight of the earth packed around them. I felt so certain they'd like to lie as they are—a part of the living vegetation and open to the sky above. Does this sound odd to you?"

131

"No," Janna said. "I feel you're right. They've lain there a long time under a blanket of nature. I think I'd prefer it that way myself."

David propped Janna on her pillows as she made grimaces of pain. He spread newspaper in her lap and handed her the volume. He carefully pried open the stiff hinges and said, "You do the honors."

Janna opened the book carefully. The writing was faded but legible. The script looked European in style but was executed in clear handwriting of someone who had been schooled in penmanship.

Janna had always loved old volumes. She read, "This is the Diary of Janis Renee Diehl" followed by the date 1732.

She and David looked at each other. "It's her diary!" Janna said. "The girl with her name carved on the banister!"

David settled down beside Janna as she read. It was late when the diary was finished.

Several times she felt she and David weren't alone. She seemed to almost glimpse two shadowy figures standing side by side as she read. Chills raced up and down her spine but she read on.

"They want us to know something," Janna said as she had begun to read. "All this time forever so long they've been trying to tell something."

As she read, it seemed she and David became the other couple—Janis and David—of a time so long ago.

She knew, Janna thought, she'd always known there was a connection to her and this house and to Janie and the house, also.

The diary unfolded their other life. She wondered about reincarnation as she read:

# THE DIARY

Jana and I thought we'd never get to be sixteen.

We spent out fifteenth year talking about 'when we're sixteen.'

When we did become sixteen we had a lovely party on the mainland. Everyone came.

The party was held on Papa's new ship.

We rather felt the ship upstaged us. The fact that we're twins usually gets us a lot of attention, but the ship was more of a marvel than we were.

As I said, dear Diary, the party was lovely and for the first time in our lives, my sister and I were allowed to stay up past twelve o'clock.

Papa now owns three large ships. The first one is named for Mamma—*Lady Nora*, the second, *The Jana* and this latter one for me, *The Janis*.

Jana and I slept late after our party but when we awoke we were eager to be sixteen.

We were a little surprised that the day went much like any other day except we had heaps of gifts from our family, friends, and Papa's business associates. That was exciting and that is where I got you, my beautiful diary. You came over from Spain on one of Papa's ships. I shall only write in you on special occasions and when something interesting happens for I don't want to fill your lovely pages with drivel.

Last night Jana and I lay in our big bed and spoke of what sixteen DIDN'T feel like.

"I suppose we have to make our own days different if sixteen is to be different," Jana declared.

Jana is always the practical of us two.

We fell asleep thinking of ways to be different. We would change our hairstyles, ask for more grown up clothing and see if we could discard our schoolgirl pinafores for dresses. We'd asked for clothing that wasn't 'twin' things.

We went to sleep happy with the prospect of being sixteen.

*

I'm back, dear diary, and something has happened to make me different, I suppose. I must tell you all about it.

Jana isn't writing in her diary, yet, but I suppose she will soon. She says nothing important enough has happened. So what happened at the beach isn't important to her. It didn't affect her the way it did me.

Here's what happened: Last week Jana and I had been hot and troublesome and underfoot a lot. We were constantly asking for the new style of dresses we decided we needed to be sixteen. We switched our hair dozens of different ways and wanted ribbons to match the dresses. We must have been different for normally Mamma was so patient. Anyway, after dinner Papa rowed back to the mainland and Mamma had some letters to write. All our kin live so far away so Mamma's letters are pretty important to her. I can't imagine what she writes about for our life is pretty well the same day by day.

Jana and I were restless, and when I asked if we could go walk along the beach and watch the silly, funny ghost crabs, Mamma let us go.

We weren't often allowed out at night alone even though the beach is just across from the house. Mamma and Papa are very involved in what's 'proper' for young girls. It restricts us from doing a lot of things I'd like to do. If we were boys we could roam about freely. When we did go out for walks alone, we were cautioned about everything—watch for snakes, don't wade deep in the water for there were currents that might suck us out, be lady-like, there seems no limit! We listen courteously, then run to the beach as fast as if we were boys. We tuck our skirts up and wade in the rolling surf. How I love it!

So Jana and I eagerly dashed down the sandy trail toward the beach. The moon was full and seemed to be up early. Darkness had not actually fully fallen. The light was silver among the deepening shadows. The sand glowed with a silver light and gentle waves lapped the shore edge in silvery lace.

As we stepped from between two large dunes and onto the beach, we froze like statues.

A large dog ran along the edge of the water and, as we watched, a tall, slender man arose from the water and walked to meet the dog.

The man was naked. I heard a quick intake of breath from Jana and saw her turn as though to leave.

Without thinking I caught her arm and held her still.

The moonlight captured him like a dark crystal against the backdrop of rolling water. He stepped upon the sand and leaned back to squeeze the water from his longish hair. As his back arched his manhood became a silhouette against the white sand beach.

My heart pounded like thunder! A warm wave surged through my body.

We had never seen a naked male and I had privately thought the sight might be rather ugly.

The man from the sea was beautiful. He whistled softly for his dog and they walked away.

Soon they were only dark shadows along the water line—they faded into indistinct blobs. He was still naked as he walked away and I wondered if I had actually seen him or if he were a dream or a God risen from the sea.

Jana whispered to me, "Do you think we should walk on the beach?"

"Maybe not tonight," I whispered back. We turned back, still whispering.

"Do you think we should tell Mamma?" Jana asked.

"Could we keep this a secret?" I asked. "If we told her, she'd tell Papa, and we could never go to the beach again." We giggled.

"Did you see IT?" Jana asked.

"Yes," I replied and we ran along the path to the house, giggling.

This all happened last night and I couldn't sleep for the longest time. Jana seemed to fall asleep quickly as we usually do.

I thought of the naked man. His form seemed youthful. I thought he was young and he evidently was a grown man. I couldn't stop thinking of how beautiful he was in the moonlight. How exciting it had been to see him naked.

When I fell asleep, I dreamed of a wonderful, tall, slender God who came to me on his chariot. We flew through the sky with his arm around me, the earth disappearing below and the stars were all around us. The wind blew back his long hair and when I looked down his manhood shone in the moonlight. I awoke at that point and I tried to recapture the dream, but it was gone. I fell back into a wonderful sleep.

Today, Jana and I giggled every time we looked at each other. Mamma asked what we were up to, and we said, "Nothing." She didn't believe us.

After dinner I asked Jana if she wanted to go to the beach again. "Do you think he'll be there?" she asked.

"Maybe," I said and we laughed together.

Mamma wouldn't let us go. We had to begin our 'thank you' notes that we had put off as long as we could. Mamma said it wasn't proper to take the presents and enjoy them so much and then be disrespectable in not thanking the people who gave them to us. Thus chided by our loving Mamma, we got busy on the notes.

*

I dreamed of him again last night. We were both naked on the beach. He took the pins out of my hair and it blew all around me in the breeze. As he was leaning to kiss me, I woke up. I lay there hungry to have the kiss. I'd never been 'kissed', of course, and neither had Jana. We know a couple of girls on the mainland who had been kissed and we were curious. The boys we knew were schoolmates that we saw only at school or at chaperoned parties or church.

I lay there wondering if I would like to kiss any of the boys I know but none of them came to mind. The man on the beach was all I

could think of.    A little thrill settled
somewhere near the pit of my stomach.

*

Today was shopping day.  We love the weekly
trip onto the mainland, to pick up staples,
have lunch with Papa if he's available and
sometimes to go to the warehouse to pick out a
few luxuries from special shipments.

Today Jana and I brought home some beautiful
Swiss organza for our new dresses.  Mamma also
picked out some nice muslin with little
flowers in different patterns.  We are going
to dress differently at last.  We can't wait
for the longer, fuller dresses.

I think Jana is the most beautiful of us
twins and she thinks I am.  Except for Mamma
and Papa, everyone thinks we are identical.
We think that's funny!

I looked everywhere today hoping to see my
dream man.  I wonder if I'd recognize him in
the daylight.  Perhaps not, but somehow I
think I would.  I didn't see him and I was
very disappointed.

*

Today Jana and I persuaded Mamma to let us
walk down to the little mercantile store on
the island.

It's a beautiful walk down the sandy road
with wild flowers, vines, and the palmettos
growing so bushy and green.

I persuaded Jana to help me get Mamma to let
us go.  Then I got her to walk back along the
beach instead of the road.  We pulled off our
shoes when we'd got some way down the beach.

We couldn't resist some of the seashells and a piece of driftwood that had a perfect weathered face on it.

I was beginning to almost believe the man was a God risen from the waters, for we'd been on the island for ten years at least and we'd never seen him before. The island is small and it seems that everyone would meet fairly often. We didn't know a lot of the island people but we saw them and they spoke to us. Papa doesn't encourage association with 'the natives', as he calls them.

I'm feeling restless. Jana and I are kept pretty close to home. We have been promised a trip to Philadelphia to see Papa's relatives and our grandparents next summer. We will stay a month after school is out. It will be our last year of school here. They are speaking of some 'finishing school' for young ladies for us in Philadelphia the following spring. Jana and I laughed at the idea for us to be 'finished'. Mamma said that Papa is from a 'good family' and they'll expect it. Also, Papa is becoming rather well to do, she said, and we need to acquire the social graces that we've been deprived of here on the island. We apparently need these social graces so we'll fit into proper society and make good marriages! I can't even imagine it! Jana and I don't really long for this finishing process.

*

I tried to dream about the man last night, but I guess you can't force dreams. It made me restless trying to dream of him, and I was still sleepy this morning when Jana bounced the bed to wake me up. We had both slept later than usual.    I guess my tossing and turning kept her from a good night of rest.

We went downstairs to breakfast and as we sat down I heard an awful banging going on behind the house.

I asked, "What is that awful racket?"

Mamma told us that Papa was having a garden room built onto the back of the house.

The workmen were there.    I looked out to see piles of lumber and materials in the back yard.

"You wanted a gazebo on the hill, Mamma. Will that be built next?" I asked her.

Mamma said that Papa was building her the porch instead because he said a hurricane would blow away the flimsy gazebo she longed for anyway.    We were disappointed but were happy to have the porch.    Our house is the nicest one on the island and we are very proud of it.

Jana and I stood looking out the back window.    Just as our noses touched the glass a head shot up just inches in front of our eyes. We gasped together.    I looked at Jana and her eyes were wide and round as an owl's.    I think mine were, too.

The man who stood up facing our window was the man from the beach.    I had no doubt.    I stared into his gold and green eyes and I felt I had looked into his soul.    Our glances held for a long moment, then I saw him do something like a doubletake as he saw me doubled in my sister standing there beside me.

Jana was blushing furiously, while I glowed with happiness.

I was overjoyed to find him at last.    He was a young man, just as I guessed, and in the light of day and clothed as well. He was still God-like.    The sun seemed to tangle in his

hair. Russet freckles matched the gold in his
eyes. His skin was tanned and his hair seemed
to have a soft shifting life of its own.

The men had worked a couple of hours and I
could see they sweated as they worked in the
hot sun. I filled a jug with cool water and
took out a cup. They thanked me for the
water. As noon approached, I asked Mamma to
fix some sandwiches from the loaf of fresh
sliced bread we had sitting in the warming
closet of the stove. We had some roast beef
and Mamma sliced it thin. She buttered one
side of the sandwich and added a thin slice of
pickle to top each slice of roast.

Jana hung back in embarrassment as I brought
out the sandwiches. I couldn't get enough of
seeing him. His voice was soft and gentle as
he thanked me.

\*

Last night Jana and I whispered and giggled
until Mamma hushed us and told us to go to
sleep.

I told Jana that I was in love.

She was horrified, then laughed until her
eyes held tears. "You're joking!" she gasped.
"Wouldn't Papa have a fit! We're going to be
FINSHED for you to marry a carpenter!" We
both laughed at that.

I took extra care dressing this morning. I
could hear hammering and voices outside when I
awoke. I wondered how long it took to build a
garden room. I hoped it would take forever.

Jana was already downstairs and beginning
breakfast when I came down.

I walked over to look out the big back
window. He was there. My heart beat
furiously. He seemed to feel my glance, for

he looked up and our eyes met. He smiled at me and lifted his hand in greeting, then was once again absorbed in his work. I watched him for a moment before turning away.

I ate breakfast swiftly, then went to fill a water jug. His back was turned from me when I brought the jug out to the yard. I realized I didn't know his name. I held the jug awkwardly then coughed softly to draw his attention. He didn't hear me so I said, "Excuse me," and he looked around.

"How wonderful," he said.

I asked, "Shall I pour you a cup?"

"I'll help you," he said to me, putting down his saw. Our fingers touched as he took the cup from me. Neither of us moved our hands for a breathless moment. Our eyes sought each other's and we spoke without words.

"I'm David," he introduced himself.

"I'm Janis," I replied.

"And so beautiful," he said holding the cup out for more water. He tipped his head back to take a long swallow. I watched the muscles move in his throat. I wanted to nuzzle my face there and kiss him. I felt myself blushing as I set the jug down and fled back to the kitchen.

I floated with the magic of his words. The day passed as though in a dream. The back window drew me often. Just before lunch I refilled the water jug for David and the other workmen. I took them out some more sandwiches from Mamma's fresh bread at lunch. I added a few cookies that Jana had cooked a couple of days ago.

We had no further conversation but David did glance at me and smile. I don't know what I did—I guess I glowed. I felt like I was glowing. I am in love and I don't care if

Jana does laugh and tease me. I don't know what to do next. Dear Diary, how can I find a way to talk to him? I have to do more than just give him water and food.

*

Oh! Joy! Mamma had to go to the mainland. Jana and I were allowed to stay home since the workmen are here. I talked to him!!!

Jana and I served some cold chicken that Mamma had fixed for the workers. When he took his lunch he sat down on a pile of boards. I brought my own piece of chicken out and popped down on the same stack of boards. I was close but not improperly close. I saw Jana's shocked face through the window.

I was close enough to see his freckles, each individual eyelash that shaded his beautiful golden flecked green eyes.

He smiled when I said, "It's coming together beautifully, don't you think?"

He asked what the purpose of the room was to be. I told him we'd sit out there to relax and to read or sew. I said we'd probably have a few couches for resting and few little tables and some chairs.

He said he noticed I read a lot. I knew he had to have seen me sitting in the kitchen with my books while I waited for the right moments to bring out water or food or to get up to look at him. So I know he was noticing me, too!

I was surprised to find he, also, loved to read! He asked if we'd like some shelves built along the inside wall to hold books and things. I suggested he ask Mamma for I didn't want her to know I had been talking to him. I knew Jana wouldn't tell. She might scold me, but she'd never tell on me.

When he rose to resume work, we exchanged long looks again. My heart was in my eyes. I'm sure he notices me in a special way. I feel it. I'm so afraid he'll finish the porch and just walk away from my life. I hope he gets to build those shelves.

When I went in, Jana was waiting for me. She was shocked, she said, at my conduct. She said I wasn't ladylike.

I love him even more.

*

I haven't written in several days. David and I are looking at each other every chance we get. I'll look out the window and somehow he knows. He will look up from his work and smile.

When I bring water out to him, our fingers touch and linger as long as we can do it and not be noticed by others. I float through these days.

I dreamed of him last night. He kissed me. It was so sweet. How can we find a way to be together? Papa would be very angry. Mamma would be shocked. I must figure some way.

*

It happened! He does like me! I walked around to the side of the front porch and was getting some sand for my potted fern. He had been out front to get some nails.

As I stood up he started to pass me by. I looked at him in the face and he paused. We stepped toward each other at the same time. One step would have put us face to face, our continuing steps put us into each other's arms.

His lips quickly brushed mine. It was like nothing I've ever felt. My heart raced, and a feeling so wonderful come over me, I couldn't feel better if I went to heaven. My heart suffocated me with excitement! We heard a footstep and parted instantly. He went, going quickly to the back of the house, and I to the front. I went in the house and was standing at the back window without feeling anything around me but the feel of his arms and kiss.

I looked hungrily out the window. He was there and our eyes met and held. I felt myself lick my lips with the tip of my tongue. He touched his, also, with the tip of his tongue as though we were tasting our quick kiss.

My first kiss was wonderful! I want more—but how?

Papa would send me to a convent if he knew. I can't even tell Jana. I'm about to explode with happiness!

*

Today when I brought out the sandwiches, David managed to whisper to me, "After we eat, meet me outside."

I nodded once as our eyes locked. I could feel heat rising from my body. I was hungry to be with him.

I ate, tasting nothing. I lingered at the table with my eyes secretly watching the window. When he rose to walk off, I got up and stretched. I walked casually to the front door and went out slowly.

Once outside I rushed off the porch and to the side of the house.

We came immediately into each other's arms. Our kiss was quick but so intense it left me trembling and pale. I felt his heart beating hard and strong through his thin shirt.

When I somehow got back inside I went to the back window and looked at him. I could see he was shaken, too.

I was so weak and excited I went upstairs and fell upon the bed to daydream about our kisses. I told Jana I was going to take a short afternoon nap. She was doing some needlework on some fancy little pillows we were making for our room.

Mamma noticed I was very quiet at dinner tonight and asked if I were all right.

Jana looked at me. Her one dimple flicked on and off quickly. I could see the merry tease in her eyes.

"Be careful," she warned me after we came to bed. "Remember our destiny: finishing school, coming out into society, and marrying, hopefully for love, and surely for money!"

"Jana!" I exclaimed, shocked, but knowing all the while that she was right.

I never had considered my future before. It was so cut and dried; it was so decided. I didn't have to think about it. Now the thought scared me. None of this could possibly include David and nothing could keep me from him.

*

I was miserable today. It's Sunday just like all of our Sundays have been. Where I looked forward to going to church and seeing my friends before, now I feel restless. I long to see David.

On the way to and from church on the mainland I sought his face in everyone we passed.

Yesterday when we met beside the house, he said, "I'll miss you tomorrow."

Our kisses have grown frantic. We want so much more than these fleeting moments that are being spent in the most exquisite desire and fear of being caught.

We must be careful for I'm afraid we'd be separated forever if we were caught.

I love him so much. I must find a way to talk to him. Our eyes and our hearts speak much but I want so much more.

\*

Monday finally came. Papa gave permission for Mamma to have bookcases built.

David will be building the bookcases alone. The other workmen won't be needed.

The porch is almost done. It is beautiful. We will sit out there and have a view of the hillside where Mamma had wanted the beautiful gazebo. We will see the bay and the outside trees and wildlife. The room is filled with windows on one side and a French door opens to the outside on the end toward the hillside. David is building the bookcases along the wall outside the kitchen window. He thinks it will take him two weeks to finish the bookcases.

I'm thinking of taking Jana in my confidence. She knows I'm mad about David. She thinks it's just an infatuation.

David and I met twice today. Nothing could be more exciting. I love the way he looks, the way he holds me, and the warmth of his lips and body as he holds me close in his arms. I even love the way he smells. "You're so beautiful!" he whispered to me today.

Thank goodness Mamma is on one of her sewing fits and her machine is upstairs on the other side of the house! She's making dresses for Jana and me from the new fabric.

Jana's dress will be trimmed in yellow. I asked to have soft green trim. Someone once said that green is the sign of life. I am so happy! Green is my color and so is blue like a beautiful blue sky.

Today David whispered, "Is there somewhere we could meet so we can talk?"

Papa would kill me, I told him, and he said, "Think of something!" as we rushed away from each other.

\*

Jana teased me today. "Do you want me to take the sandwiches out today?" she asked.

Mamma was in the kitchen and I passed a frown in Jana's direction.

"I'm used to doing it," I said and grabbed up the plate.

Mamma has a sixth sense; she must have heard something funny in our voices for she turned to look at us.

I felt myself start to blush as I turned to go outside with the plate of food. "Be careful," I whispered as I offered the plate to David. "Mamma may be watching."

"I'll see you later. Signal me," he said under his breath.

I hurried back inside. I couldn't wait for Mamma to go back upstairs to sew.

I was upset when she asked Jana and me to come upstairs to her sewing room with her so she could fit us for our new dresses.

It was late before I could find a private moment, and as I rushed back around the house after a quick kiss and a precious moment, Jana stood by the door.

She saw me dash around the house and practically leap onto the porch.

"What were you doing?" she asked.

"I thought I dropped something when I got sand for the fern the other day," I said.

Jana said nothing and I felt awful. She and I have never lied to each other.

After we went to bed I told her the truth—all of it.

She was shocked, then very curious.

"You know you can't see him after this job is over, and I think if Mamma and Papa found out there'd be an awful time of it. David can't fit into your life. Look at him, Janis. He usually goes shoeless and when he does wear shoes, they are those rubber fisherman's boots. He'd never be able to support you, and he isn't socially acceptable. I wish you'd stop while you can," she said to me with tears in her eyes. I was sad to see my sister cry. I hugged her and said to her, "He is my soul."

*

When I took the plate of ham and bread out today, Jana looked as though she'd faint. I was afraid Mamma would notice the way she was acting. I knew she was afraid for me.

Later I asked Jana to listen for me when I met David. She was to step out on the porch and cough real loud if Mamma started downstairs.

David had only brought one workman with him and he assigned him a task that would occupy him while we met.

149

We had about ten minutes together.

I was so weak after our kisses that I could hardly stand. I could feel David's heart hammering against my body. I never knew love could be like this. I know why Jana doesn't understand. She is where I was before I met David, before I saw him on the beach. I think these feelings started for him then. I think we were put on this earth for each other. Of course, Jana saw him that night, too, and she felt nothing but shock. She just giggled with me about seeing a naked man there in the moonlight.

It was something so special for me, and nothing but a curiosity for her.

It is as though my life stepped out from the ocean, there in the moonlight. It was like some sort of baptism in which a new me was born.

\*

Mamma had to have more ribbon from the mercantile store on the mainland. I asked Jana to accompany her and I pleaded having my womanly time of the month and a cramping stomach. The first part was true.

Jana told Mama she wanted to look at some threads for her needlepoint.

Mamma fixed me some of the herb tea she always fixes us for the cramps and told me to drink it and go to bed until I felt easier.

I kissed Mamma on the cheek and Jana rolled her eyes behind her back. I was sorry to trick Mamma, but I knew I couldn't tell her without losing David.

I thought Mamma and Jana would never leave. I ran to the upper window of our bedroom and looked over the bay.

I saw the ferry sail and could make out Mamma's blue cloak and Jana's scarlet one. I literally ran outside!

David was alone today, finishing up the trim around the screens. When he found out we were all alone he was overjoyed.

We decided to go to the parlor so we could watch for anyone approaching. David could sprint for the back of the house and me to the front door.

We opened the drapes just a slit and settled on the divan.

We forgot to watch and were soon lost on a trip to heaven in each other's arms. I could feel David's manhood against my leg as he lay over me. I was surprised it felt so hard and inflexible—I had imagined it different.

My head cradled in his arms and our lips and tongues did breathtaking things to each other. We didn't talk much for we couldn't get enough of each other. Time flew by on wings of ecstasy. We were literally gasping for breath and almost overcome with desire when we heard Jana laughing loudly and Mamma's soft response.

We sprang apart. David disappearing to the back and I up the stairs. I knew I couldn't go to the door as planned. My hair had fallen from its pins and was wildly streaming down my back. My dress was wet with perspiration and a wrinkled mess. I jumped under the coverlet on the bed and buried my face in my pillow. I tried to bring my harsh breathing to a more normal rate. My heart was still beating from both desire and fear. I could hear Jana and Mamma climbing the stairs and the door opened to our room.

Jana whispered, "Janis?" and I sat up. "You look a mess!" Jana whispered. I reached up to take the pins from my hair, which had been pinned into a neat coil at the nape of my neck when Jana had left. It was now hanging loose in wild tangles. I rushed to the dresser and was brushing my hair when Mamma came in. "Did you have a nice rest, dear?" she asked.

"Yes, Mamma," I replied, not daring to glance toward Jana. I could feel Jana's look. After we went up to bed I told Jana what had happened. She is scared for me but I can trust her. She'd never tell. She just isn't able to understand.

"He'll be gone in a week or so," she said, still thinking that when the work was done that would be the end of it. I said nothing.

****** 

Mamma was trying to finish our dresses for Sunday so she was in her sewing room much of the afternoon. Jana watched while I spoke with David. He was working alone again so we had only one direction to watch and Jana was covering that.

David asked if I thought he should ask Pappa if he could court me. I explained to him what Pappa's plans for Jana and I included. All happiness drained from David's face.

"I love you so much I hadn't thought that far. Of course I'm not good enough for you. Your Pappa's right. You deserve and need more than I could ever give you. You should see the place where I live—and it isn't even mine. I don't have anything but an aunt and an uncle who love me, and a happy life with them. The house is small, not a mansion like this. We have plenty of food, a roof over our heads that thanks to me doesn't leak. We have screens on our windows, which most of our friends don't and we have mosquito netting over our beds, which most of our friends don't have either. We have the island with it's beautiful beach. We have the gulf and it's bounty, which provides us with wonderful food. I've never considered myself poor or inferior or inadequate—until now."

Tears swam in David's eyes and also in mine. He turned to go and I caught his arm.

"David," I said to him, "that's what PAPPA wants. That's why you can't ask to court me. What I say is that I love you. I'll NEVER marry anyone else. I want YOU. I'd love to meet your wonderful family. I'd love to go to your house. I care NOTHING for wealth and society. They are empty pursuits without love or happiness. I have found you and you are my world. I'm only sixteen. When I'm seventeen I'm to go to Philadelphia. I won't be going. I can't upset my family right now. I will see you, somehow, if you'll allow me to and we will plan our life together for this is where I belong and this is where I will stay."

David reached out and touched my face. I leaned into his warm, moist palm and found myself in his arms.

"Are you sure, Janis?" he asked. "Life here is not always easy. There are few fine things for us natives."

"You are my luxury," I smiled at him and his lips touched mine. We were lost in each other when I became aware that Jana was coughing desperately. I heard Mamma's voice on the front porch asking Jana what was wrong.

David and I fled as silently as we could. I dashed in through the new garden room and ran upstairs to our room. I heard David hammering on some boards. "We've got to be more careful," I thought.

Jana was calling from downstairs. "I'm here!" I answered from the top of the stairs.

Jana shook her fist at me. Mamma came up behind her. "Oh! There you are!" she said. "I want you and Jana to try on your dresses."

By the time we got back downstairs David was gone. I knew we had passed an important part of our lives. It was as though we had become betrothed. I was sad that my parents couldn't be a part of my happiness. I was grateful. though, that Jana was my confidante, though I held back what had taken place between David and me today.

**\* \* \* \* \* \***

David has worked on the bookcases all this week. We met each day briefly. I even sat on the new porch swing and watched him place shelves along the inner wall of the new room. I took a book outside with me and pretended to read. Mamma came out for awhile and complimented the work he was doing.

"Janis, don't annoy the young man," she cautioned. "She's inspiration, ma'am," he replied. She laughed. He and I talked quietly. I found out he likes to read, and found he had read many of the same classics.

"My aunt taught me to read," he said, "when she was the only school teacher this island. Some of the island children never learned to read and as adults they still don't. Reading has been my salvation."

Being able to sit and watch David work and to talk to him was better than courting. We didn't have to sit stiffly in the parlor or on the front porch, as we would if we were officially courting. The difference in our ages and stations in life was working in this case. The days were heaven.

"Whatever do you find to talk to him about?" Jana asked.

"Why, just EVERYTHING!," I answered her. She looked surprised.

Today David brought me a book. It was one that he'd mentioned, and that I hadn't read. He asked Mamma if it were all right if he loaned it to me. She looked it over and smiled at him.

"It's been a long time since I've read this. Janis will love it," she said.

"It is one of my aunt's books," he said.

I told Mamma she had been the only school teacher on the island when he was growing up.

"Do you enjoy reading?" Mamma asked.

"Very much," he replied.

"Then when our books are placed on these beautiful shelves you've built you will be welcome to look them over and borrow from us as well. Our books are almost all in crates in the attic. We've just not had a place to display them until now."

David offered to help bring down the books when the shelves were ready.

"Two more days and this will all be complete," he said, and I felt him glance toward me.

Each day I'm happier than the last. Jana just can't understand it. It's as though I'm growing up and she's staying a younger girl.

\*\*\*\*\*\*

David slipped a letter to me when we met beside the house to hold each other and kiss. I will keep the letter always. The letter was so sweet.

Jana says that I don't act like a lady, and that nice young girls don't meet men behind their parents' backs. She said that I will break Mamma and Pappa's hearts if I'm not careful. She says I'll bring shame and disgrace on all of us if I keep on. She even said she is glad the job is about to end.

I told her that I'd love him forever.

"You can't," she replied.

\*\*\*\*\*\*

Today we brought the books down from the attic. I have persuaded Mamma to let me catalogue and alphabetize them with David's help. I thought my heart would leap out of my body I was so excited.

Today was the loveliest yet. David and I worked on the 'library' all day. Stars could not have outshone our eyes. We stacked the books in stacks according to their author's alphabetical order. Then we listed them and put them on the shelves.

Tomorrow we will be finished and we're going to try to meet on the beach if Mamma will let Jana and I go walking after dinner in the early evening.

David will leave his next job and go straight to the beach and wait for me if I'm not there. We also plan to exchange books since Mamma offered. We will find a safe place to leave letters to each other.

We have been desperate to think of ways to see and hear from each other. Jana will have a fit but I know she will help me.

\*\*\*\*\*\*

Today was David's last day here at the house.

Mamma went to the mainland for her latest sewing project. She has decided we need new petticoats and underthings. All of our chemises are too tight and our petticoats are getting too short. Jana and I have grown a lot these past two years. It seems we're going to be rather tall and maybe very pretty.

David says I'm beautiful.

Mamma left Jana behind with me and she stayed to herself.

David and I found ways to touch each other and to kiss until we were both weak and trembling.

Why can't life be simple? If I could wish any wish I wanted, I would wish to marry David—now—with no fuss; just a simple wedding and to be free to laugh, love and be near him always. I would be happy for the rest of my life.

Why does power and money and social prestige have to rule my life? I care nothing for it. I feel like a piece of merchandise—of no more worth than the bolts of silk that come in on the ships or some other piece of expensive merchandise. My life is to be for sale to the highest bidder in Philadelphia society. I won't have it!

David is my soul. I could never find the courage to tell Pappa. He'd send me away. I know he would. Mamma might understand somewhat but she'd think I don't know what's best for me and she'd side with Pappa.

I must prepare myself for breaking my parent's hearts for when the time comes to go to Philadelphia next year I won't go.

I have so much happiness and so much sadness in my heart living there side by side and in constant war. I never doubt David is my true and only love.

It rained this afternoon. The rain was hard, lightning streaked and dark clouds rushed across the angry sky. There was no chance to go to the beach to see David. I missed him today.

I read the book he loaned me. I loved it as he thought I would. I've written a letter to pass along with his book when I return it. Maybe Jana is right and I'm not ladylike. I poured my heart out to him in the letter. I don't think we have time for those little time-consuming niceties of courtship. I somehow feel David and I have never had to go through those 'getting acquainted' rituals. We've always known each other. We will always know each other. I shiver when I think of how he rose from the sea—as though the sea gave birth to him, naked and beautiful, there in the moonlight.

**\* \* \* \* \* \***

It rained all day again today. I feel like running out in the downpour to find David, to hold him, and kiss him and feel his body through his wet clothes. My breath comes fast as I visualize David and I, wet and clinging to each other.

Jana thinks the job's over and so is David. I will have to tell her how involved I am soon for I'll need her help.

She doesn't understand love. I think until you find it (if you're lucky enough to find real love) then you can't know what it is.

I know about love and Jana doesn't.

**\* \* \* \* \* \***

This morning the sun came out and steam rose into wisps like tiny clouds. The play of the sunlight on the sparkling greenery, and the trailing wisps of mist, was enchanting.

I sat in the garden room after breakfast and daydreamed.

The sunlight continued throughout the day. The many birds on the island were rapturous in song and search of food. The bay sparkled beyond the hill at the back of the house.

Tiny squirrels scampered in and out of the thick vines that twined every where. Little blue butterflies swarmed over the jungle-like growth out back. They especially hovered over the hill.

I drank in the beauty and went to the door, opened it and drew in lungfuls of fresh air. I could hear the soft roar of the rolling gulf and see the gulls in lazy flight as they lay upon the breeze.

I love the island and have never wanted to live anywhere else. The infrequent trips we'd taken to Iowa where Mamma was raised, and Philadelphia where Pappa had all those rich relatives, were never pleasant for me.

The cities were confusing and noisy. I felt suffocated in them. The flat fields of grain in Iowa left me longing for the beautiful sparkling waters of the gulf and the lush green vegetation of the island. The crows were noisy irksome birds, not like the graceful gulls, the pelicans with their formation and swift dives, or the skinny-legged little birds that ran along the beach. The herons were magnificent birds and all the songs of the combination of songbirds were like music to me. The cawing of the crows was an ugly sound. Mamma was always very happy when she visited Iowa, but she had been raised there.

Pappa had defied custom when he'd married the beautiful girl from an Iowa farm. Mamma's parents were prosperous farmers, but still farmers.

Philadelphia had been a nightmare for Mamma at first, she admitted to Jana and me. She had kept smiling, been as charming as she could manage and in a few years she'd felt more comfortable. Just as she was adapting to the Philadelphia society, Pappa purchased his first ship and they'd moved to 'the wilds of Florida' as Mamma put it. Mamma had once again made her adjustments.

Jana and I were six years old when we left Philadelphia and moved to the island.

The beach, the gulf's waves, the sea shells, and the birds enchanted me. I loved the warmth.

When I think of Philadelphia I think of cold. I've always hated the cold weather. Jana is more adaptable to cold than me. She is more like Mamma. I'm not sure who I'm like.

Today Mamma let Jana and me go for a stroll along the beach. She has always encouraged exercise.

David was there.

I had brought along the letter I'd written and I slipped it to him while Jana's head was turned away. The three of us walked along the water's edge. It was so special.

Jana finally had an opportunity to speak with David. They seemed to talk well together and I was glad. I want her to see him as an intelligent, wonderful man-not just 'a native'.

I walked close beside David. Our hands touched and clung briefly at times. His arm brushed or pressed against mine. It was maddening not to be able to hold him.

Jana has no idea our meeting David wasn't an accident. I'll have to tell her soon.

******

Yesterday it rained, today it rained, tomorrow is Sunday. If the sun doesn't shine by Monday, I don't know what I'll do.

I miss David so much. I've been trying to read and Jana has a fit of piano playing going on. She is really a dreadful piano player and her banging even got to Mamma once.

******

Monday and the sun was weak, but out. Mamma let us walk on the beach. She said we were getting to be like caged animals and a brisk walk along the beach would be beneficial.

I wore my blue ribbons in my hair and my sprigged blue muslin dress. Jana wore yellow of the same pattern.

As we approached the beach my heart was pounding. I was heartbroken to find David wasn't there. Jana and I were about to return to the house when he came running along the beach.

I was so happy.

"Must you go?" he asked.

"We can't stay much longer," I said, "it's late and Mamma will be concerned." The sun had almost set, drawing the glorious colors that had spread along the waters back to herself.

"The sun's like a fisherman," David said. "She casts out her net of colors and draws them back in slowly. The silhouettes will soon be prancing onto land and after they've played 'guess what I am?', night falls."

"That's beautiful, David," I said to him. "You're wonderfully poetic." Silhouettes were just approaching in the distance when Jana pulled me away from the beach. David's hand squeezed mine and we looked into each other's eyes. A fat fold of papers slid into my hand and I quickly hid them in the folds of my skirt.

"And was this meeting an accident, too?" Jana asked. I laughed and we raced for the house. Mamma was lighting the lamps.

I crept down to the porch after everyone was asleep. I had hidden my letter behind the cover of a large book and I took it out and read David's wonderful words of love and desire for us to be together. I've had an idea tonight, but I have to determine whether I have the courage to follow it or not.

**\* \* \* \* \* \***

I haven't seen David in a couple of days. One day was because of the weather and the other day was last night, when Pappa asked Mamma to bring us to the mainland, to meet a new family in the shipping business. Jana and I were thrilled to meet the two daughters, who must be close to our age, and the son who was perhaps a year older. Alice, Nancy and Jared were all blond-haired, with large blue eyes and dark lashes. They looked like three beautiful overgrown dolls.

All three were fun and Jared was quite mischievous. I think Jana was attracted to him. We had a great evening but I still missed David. Jared was impeccably dressed. I couldn't help comparing him to David and I loved David even more. There is nothing doll-like about David. He is so very real.

\*\*\*\*\*\*

I saw David today. My heart almost stopped when Mamma answered a tap on the door and David stood there. He had returned a book I had loaned him and he had another of his Aunt's books for me to read.

Mamma looked the hook over saying, "This is quite lovely. I've never read this. Do you think your aunt would mind if I read it, also?"

David was so pleased at Mamma's reaction to the book. He fairly beamed with pleasure. I stepped up beside her and asked David if he'd like to look over our books and borrow another one.

He asked Mamma if it would be all right. "Why certainly!" she said and then she had me take him out to the garden room to select something. We found a chance for a quick kiss.

"I just HAD to see you," David said.

"I know, I felt the same," I said and then I told him quite boldly of my plan so we could be together.

"What if your Pappa catches us?" he asked.

"I think he'd send me to some convent up east," I answered him.

"Then we can't take too many chances," David said. "Let's set certain days—perhaps three days a week that way and try the beach walks with Jana the other days."

"Except Sunday," I said and he answered, "Yes, except Sundays."

We decided to start tomorrow night. I'll sneak out after everyone is asleep and we'll meet between the tall dunes just off the beach pathway. I am so excited I'm trembling already with anticipation.

163

******

It was late last night when I crept from the house with a wildly beating heart, fearing with each step. I hadn't realized I'd be so terrified as I crept down the stairs and out through the garden room door, along the side of the house then fled down the path toward the dunes.

David sat beside the large dune just before the beach. He and I were immediately in each other's arms. This was the private time we'd yearned for so desperately. David's lips were so soft, so sweet, so full of love and then our kisses changed. We were both flaming with desire for each other. David was the one who pulled back. I couldn't. I never knew what wanting to fulfill our relationship as a man and woman was, until this night. Everything I'd felt before paled before the fires of my desire for David.

We gained control of ourselves, then began kissing again. It seemed as though we were standing one moment and lying beside each other in the sand the next. We lay in the sand kissing and holding each other from top to toe. Every body part we had seemed connected. Our bodies began a rhythm between them and we fed our bodies of each other through our clothing. We pushed ourselves against each other and rocked together, our breath coming in gasps and our lips devouring each other—again David pushed me aside.

"No," he moaned. "No, we have to slow down. I think you'd better go back now before we're in trouble."

"Can we still meet this way?" I asked him and he said, "I can't refuse."

"Then is the day after tomorrow okay—after they are all asleep?" I asked, my voice husky with desire.

We had fun brushing the sand from my hair and body. Even that was very exciting.

**\* \* \* \* \* \***

The days have gone slowly and the nights have flown by. I haven't written to you, dear diary, in weeks and I know you must wonder what's happening. (Silly me.)

Jana has been complaining of sand in our bed. She's woke up several times to find I'm not in the room. I told her I often sneaked downstairs at night to read and that a few times I'd walked on the beach in the moonlight.

"Aren't you afraid?" she asked. I told her "no".

"Pappa will put you in a nunnery before you're eighteen!" she predicted. "He'll be insane if he knew you went out walking alone at night!"

"I HAVE to be free!" I told her. "I feel like a caged animal. I feel like I'm to be fatted for the kill—or rather like I'm being groomed for sale to the highest bidder. We have so little time left, Jana, to live here on the island."

"I know," Jana said, and then confessed she wasn't as anxious as she'd once been to go out into the world.

We had become better acquainted with Alice, Nancy and Jared. Jared was eighteen and being prepared for a position in his father's company after college. He and Jana had become close and I even heard Mamma and Pappa discussing the possibility of a future match between them some day.

How I wish it were possible for David and me! How I hate 'social position'; that awful hypocrisy that keeps David and me apart and wants to place me instead in the bed of someone I'd detest.

It's evil—an evil that forces us to have to sneak out to be together and lie between the dunes to love and perspire and have sand stick to our skin and hair.

David brought a coverlet along to keep the sand from my hair and clothing.

Mamma has noticed how much sand some of my clothing held and I dug about in the yard for a few days and put new sand and soil in my plants I've been accumulating for the garden room. I made sure she saw how sandy I got.

David and I undressed last night. He has long since been free to touch then kiss my breasts. We ran naked into the gulf and played.

The warm waves nudged us and rolled about us in moonlit splendor. The sky was dripping with stars and a soft warm breeze moved like sheets of satin over our bodies.

We held each other and David's naked manhood bobbed stiffly between my legs. He moved closer and I pressed it between my thighs.

I wanted more but David wouldn't.

"Your fancy husband will expect a virgin," he said, "and I love you too much to spoil you."

"YOU are the only fancy husband I ever want," I told him. I thought I saw tears on his face, but it may have been the wetness from the waters gleaming on his cheeks and glazing his beautiful eyes.

His voice held such sadness as he said, "How I wish that were possible. I love you, Janis and I'll love you forever, but your parents will win in the long run. This, right here, is all we have. This is as far as we can go. "It's so beautiful. You're so beautiful. I'll remember this for as long as I live and maybe beyond. Nothing and no one will ever replace these nights and my love for you."

We stayed too long. The moon was close to surrendering to the sun rise when I rushed back home and tip-toed upstairs. My heart was beating wildly with every creak the floor made.

My hair was still wet and I knew there'd be trouble if I encountered anyone. I knew I looked a mess. I undressed hurriedly and crawled under the covers with Jana.

**\* \* \* \* \* \***

Again, weeks have passed.

So much has happened that sometimes I can't seem to share it with anyone, not even you, Dear Diary.

This has to be told. I'm bursting with joy.

Last night I lost my virginity to David.

I forced him to have me. I would hate to have any other man take my maidenhood. It had to be David and no other.

He was so sweet and gentle and it didn't hurt much at all. He told me what to expect.

I never want to let him go. I will love him forever and they'll have to tear me from his arms if I'm ever taken away.

David wants to marry me and I, of course, want to marry him.

Sometimes I'm tempted to tell Mamma that I love him, but I know Pappa won't let me marry him and Mamma will go along with Pappa's decision. She'll say it's for the best, that someday I'll realize it myself.

My heart has sung David's name all day.

It's so bittersweet loving him. It's as though each time we're together might be the last. We treasure each minute we're together.

I can't wait to feel his wonderful arms holding me close again. I'm a woman now and I'm so in love.

**\* \* \* \* \* \***

David and I are wild together. We can't get enough of each other. We make love until we're weak and then we dive naked into the gulf. David has taught me to swim. It's a wonderful feeling.

Jana had cautioned me to be careful. I think she suspects that I sneak out to walk with David.

David and I spoke private marriage vows and we are now married in the sight of God—or so we believe. I wish we could have had a wedding blessed by my family and the community.

The night was both so incredibly sweet and so sad. We made love so tenderly and completely. Afterward we danced on the beach as the waves made our music and the stars above reflected upon the water, dancing with the rhythm of the waves. It was almost dawn before we could tear ourselves apart.

**\* \* \* \* \* \***

Dear Diary, I am so grateful I have you. David and I have a secret that only you can know. I have missed three menstrual cycles. I told David last night.

We are both happy and frightened. I look the same except my breasts seem to be firmer and more sensitive. I don't know much about babies, but I'm happy.

David is afraid of Pappa and so am I. Maybe they'll let us marry. Now I won't have to be presented to high society—I'm ruined and I'm glad.

David and I would have done the proper courting, gone through the proper engagement, and had the proper marriage if we'd been given the chance. We'd have waited until I was eighteen even, but we weren't given those choices.

I love him so much. All day I've smiled as I've thought of our baby growing inside of me.

\*\*\*\*\*\*

David is so gentle with me. He handles me like a glass figurine.

We talk about our baby a lot. When I begin to show I'll tell Mamma. I don't want to spoil this happiness.

I'm beginning to show my pregnancy a bit but it's hidden under my full skirts. Jana noticed it last night. "We're not exactly the same size anymore," she said.

"I think I eat too much and don't walk enough," I told her.

"You are a piggy at the table!" she teased for I'd always eaten more than Jana.

\*\*\*\*\*\*

I've had to finally tell Jana I'm around six months pregnant.

Mamma has cautioned me to eat less so I'll not be fat. "Men like small waists," she said, "and you're out of control, Honey. You've split a couple of seams, and I think you'll need a larger size than Jana wears now."

Mamma began new pinafores for us the next day. She had found some new material in Pappa's warehouse and had liked it so much she'd brought it home, planning to sew us new clothes later.

******

I've tried to eat less but I get so hungry. I am eating for two and I should take care of my baby inside me by staying healthy, David said.

He loves my big stomach. He kisses it and talks to our baby and I love it when he does.

Mamma has finished our new pinafores and when she fitted me she had a tiny frown between her eyes. I am much more comfortable in my new dresses.

I think I'm into my seventh month of pregnancy.

I told Jana last night and she cried. I told her how happy I am and told her the whole story.

"You know you've disgraced the family," she said, crying harder.

"No, Jana," I told her. "The family has disgraced me." "I never wanted to leave this island. I never wanted to marry the 'right' man in the 'right' social position and for wealth instead of love. I met David and I loved him immediately and will for forever. Pappa would never have let us court, in fact, he'd have sent me away. He'd have sent us BOTH away—you, too."

Jana held me and we both cried. "You're right about Pappa," she said.

\* \* \* \* \* \*

I'm approaching my eight month of pregnancy and Mamma has asked Jana if I might have been alone with some boy at some time. Jana was terrified. She said that Mama had to have seen her fear.

My breasts are large and tender and under the new full skirts my stomach is round as a melon. It seems to grow daily. David kisses the big round stomach that looks like a huge white balloon in the moonlight when we pull off our clothes there among the sand dunes and walk along the beach.

I was shy to take my clothes off after my stomach got large, but David said I'm even more beautiful than ever. He whispers sweet nonsense to the baby inside my stomach. He will be such a good Pappa to our child.

David said he wants to tell his aunt about the baby and I've given him permission.

His aunt is also the island midwife. I wish I could talk to her. I know nothing about babies and childbirth. The few things I've heard were spoken in whispers and considered unfit conversation for children's ears. I've gathered that it hurts awfully, but once it's over the pain is worth it, and is actually forgotten in the joy of having the tiny baby. I hope this is true.

\* \* \* \* \* \*

Mamma called me into her room today. I was frightened and tears ran down my cheeks as I told her about David and our wish to be married.

Mamma's face was as white as paste. "Pappa will KILL him!" she whispered. "You're a

CHILD! How dare he violate you! You're disgraced, Janis! Whatever shall we do?"

Mamma sat for awhile looking as though she were deep in thought. "Who else knows?" she finally asked. "Has David told anyone, possibly bragged to his friends?"

"No," I told her, and then I said, "We're married." "What priest presumed to take on the responsibility with you so young and without the blessing of your Pappa or his permission?" she asked. "Who would DARE!" she asked, her face now longer white but flushed red. Her eyes scared me. I had somehow expected her comfort, not this. I had never seen Mamma upset like that.

I told her of our private vows and told her that David had wanted to ask Pappa's permission to court me and I wouldn't let him. I told her how I'd been the one to make every advance and every decision.

"Have you no shame?" she asked me.

"I love him with my very soul and I'll love him forever," I said. "I have lived in fear of being sent away from the island. I have NEVER wanted to go to Philadelphia. Never wanted to marry for money instead of love. I don't WANT a society life.

"Surely you can understand that, Mamma. You know how happy you are when you go back to Iowa. I would die if I had to live in a cold, hateful place like Philadelphia and be away from the sunshine and the beautiful water. I hate the city. I love the plants, the sand and the sound of the waves of the gulf.

"I hate the barren streets and sound of the buggies and carts and people all bunched up so close and going, going, all the time. I don't like those endless fields and farms in Iowa very much either—but I'd like Iowa much more than Philadelphia, just as you do." I realized I was running on endlessly as I reached up to wipe away the tears that were running down my face.

"I belong here and David and I belong together," I said.

Mamma reached out and pulled me down to sit beside her. She pulled open the drawer in the table by the bed and handed me one of her lacy little handkerchiefs.

"Even so, Janis," she said, "your Pappa will blame me for this and no decent man will want you now."

I couldn't believe Mamma had said that after all I'd told her. Was she still thinking they'd try to palm me off on some society fool, some man I'd never love? My mind reeled at the thought.

"David IS a decent man and HE wants me!" I said. I turned and left the room.

I stayed in my room through lunch. Jana brought me up some food. Her eyes were red from weeping. After Pappa came in that night I heard him yelling. I could, also, hear Mamma. Her voice sounded hysterical, not at all like her normal self.

The fact that Mamma was hysterical made it even more frightening. My baby moved around as though agitated. I patted it through my stomach to try to comfort it. I hoped it understood.

Pappa's rage seemed endless. Finally Jana crept up to our room.

"Jana, what's happening?" I asked.

"Pappa has gone berserk. He's blaming Mamma, me, David, and you. He's raving mad. He wants to kill David or have some of his sailors beat him to death and throw him to the sharks!

"He's trying to figure to keep your pregnancy hidden. He still plans to marry us off to Philadelphia society. He wants to send you away and secretly adopt out the baby. He wants the three of us, you, Mamma and me, to take a ship to Europe and to come back without the baby. Then you and I are to go to finishing school.

"He wants Mamma to keep you out of sight until the arrangements can be made. He doesn't want to see you this way. You're to be kept from his sight. He's going to get us off this island and out of this country as soon as possible."

All of this gushed from Jana's mouth as I sat transfixed with horror. I was tearless from the shock. Jana sat beside me on the bed shaking with sobs. I reached out and held her in my arms as well as I could with my big stomach between us.

"This is much worse than I could ever imagine," I said. I patted Jana until her sobs died away. "I'm sorry this has made you suffer, Jana," I said sadly. "You know, I'm at least eight months pregnant now. How can Pappa possibly be considering such a plan? Suppose I have the baby on the ship? Suppose I die?"

Jana clutched my hand. "Then what can we DO?" she asked. I reached out and took her hand. I placed it on my stomach.

"What was THAT?" she asked in horror. "Are you going to have it NOW!"

"No," I even managed to laugh. "It's the baby kicking. It's saying, 'hello, Aunt Jana!'" Jana was awestruck. She sort of rubbed my stomach and the baby moved again.

"Does it hurt when it does that?" she asked.

"No, it's like butterflies stirring about—or some sort of indescribable feeling of knowing that my baby is alive and growing, and it spreads joy throughout me when it stirs that way."

"Listen, Jana," I told her. "David has told me that his aunt is a midwife. She knows about the baby now. I want Mamma to know about her, in case I begin to give birth. Now I'm really scared. I had thought she would be there to help me. I don't think Mamma could handle it."

Jana and I fell asleep curled up together as though for safety. It was the way we'd slept when we were very small.

****** 

I was ill when I woke up. Jana went downstairs and brought up toasted bread and milk. I managed to hold it down but I had to go back to bed.

Hours later I heard someone at the door and it was Mamma.

"I'm sorry you're ill, child, but we have to talk," she said. Her eyes were reddened and I knew she'd been crying.

"Pappa is making some plans and has set down some rules that you must obey," she said, her eyes straying out the window and not meeting mine. She went on to say, "You've disgraced yourself and our family. This will affect all of us. Here's what your Pappa and I plan: Pappa is making arrangements for you to be admitted to a small clinic in Europe. You will have the baby there.

"Jana, you and I will go by ship and then travel inland only a short distance.

"Pappa's sister, Aunt Hortense, who eventually died of consumption, went there several times for the fresh sea air and to rest.

"It's been rumored that well-to-do young ladies who want to be discreet are cared for there, also. Hortense verified this, as she had met a couple of wealthy foreign girls who were 'enciente'.

"We will stay there until the baby is adopted and you are well enough to travel back. You will not be coming back to the island. Until Pappa makes these arrangements you'll stay home. I realize we don't have much time. A first baby can come either late or early.

"I've begun an order for proper clothing for the trip. We'll need much different clothing than what we wear here on the island. We'll need heavier clothing on the ship. We've not needed heavy cloaks here, nor heavier fabric for our clothing. We live very simply here. As you know from our few trips to Philadelphia, it's not so simple in places where there are more people. We must have hats, gloves, and numerous items in a hurry. I shall be quite busy with all of this, with the help of your Pappa."

Mamma had moved to sit beside me during this horrifying account of the plans she and Pappa had made. She rose to go, saying, and still not really looking at me, "Do you understand all I've said to you, Janis?"

"Yes," I answered, my heart was like lead. "Don't I have anything to say about this?" I asked. "I don't want to leave this island and I want to marry David and keep our child!"

"That's not possible," Mamma said. "There's your Pappa's business to consider, the relatives, Jana and our family in general. You've disgraced us all. We've got to keep this quiet!"

Mamma looked at my stomach and I could see something like a frown run across her face as though she'd been struck. After she left the room Jana came in.

"What did she say?" she asked. Tears streamed down my face.

"It's as you said and even worse!" I managed to say.

****** 

I cried off and on all night. I tried to be as still and quiet as possible to keep Jana from being disturbed.

I finally got up and sat at our desk. I lit a candle and wrote to David. I told him the whole story. I asked him to help me find a solution for I don't intend to go away from him and this island.

Just as I was finishing the letter I heard the door opening slowly. I quickly tried to hide the letter but Pappa was faster than me. He snatched it from my fingers. Pages fell to the floor. I'm not as supple as I was before my stomach grew. Pappa had gathered them up by the time I squatted to try to retrieve them.

"This had better not be what I think it is!" Pappa bellowed. His face scared me. He rushed from the room with my heartfelt letter to David in his hand.

Jana was sitting up in bed, the covers clutched to her chest and her eyes round with fear.

"I was trying to explain to David," I cried out in anguish. My sobbing shook my whole body. Jana filled a glass of water from the ewer beside our bed. She brought it to my lips and patted me with her other hand.

"Hush, hush, hush," she crooned as though I were a small child. I drank the water and leaned against her. When I had stopped shaking so hard Jana half lifted me saying, "Come to bed, Janis. I'll find a way to help you. I promise."

We lay close together and spoke in whispers. I told her how I was sure David still waited by the dunes in the evenings. She planned to sneak out to talk to him at her first opportunity. In the meanwhile, I could write a letter in the afternoons while Mamma sewed. She'd take it to leave for David to find.

I finally fell asleep with a small measure of hope. I know Jana will be true to her promise and it's that promise that I cling to desperately.

**\* \* \* \* \* \***

I was very nervous as I wrote to David. Even the baby didn't stir within my body, as though it were being quiet and listening with me. I sat in bed writing on my little portable writing desk. I was careful not to get ink on the snowy linen coverlet and sheets. I wanted no attention directed toward my writing materials, for I knew they might be taken away at any time.

I began to hide you, dear diary, for I can no longer feel you're safe from Pappa's hands. He would tear out your dear pages of the story of David and of our love for each other.

I listened for the boards to creak in the hallway should anyone approach. I had the pillows arranged to slide my little writing desk under and to thus hide every indication of my continued writing from sight. I would quickly feign sleep if I was fast enough.

Mamma avoided me as much as possible. When I did see her I saw traces of weariness on her face. She was no longer the warm, wonderful Mamma I had known. It was as though a stranger had taken over her body. She was trying to add to our wardrobe for the trip. Many things were ordered and she was trying to get the rest done herself as quickly as possible.

Jana said she was sewing soft woolen dresses with little jackets over them. Mine were dark maroon and a dark blue. Jana's were of lighter colors. She was also sewing long fringe on large cashmere squares for long shawls for us to wear aboard the ship. Mine would help hide my stomach as well as to keep me warm.

I was planning to sneak out after everyone slept. If David wasn't there, I planned to hide somewhere until I could find him. I was desperate.

Thank goodness that Jana was able to sneak out my letter. She came dangerously close to being caught.

After Jana had crept out the garden room door to take my letter to the dunes, I heard Pappa come in. He had been out late every night and had come in well after we were all in bed. Jana had counted on this but he had come in earlier. I was stiff with fear when I heard him come in.

His big voice that I used to love boomed up the stairs. I heard Mamma in the hallway greeting him and listened with quaking heart to him ascending the stairs.

I looked wildly about. I quickly stuffed blankets under the covers on Jana's side of the bed. It was dark inside the room with only a very faint illumination coming in from the window. I molded the blankets to look like a curled up figure at rest, or so I hoped. He and Mamma spoke and they passed on into their bedroom. I heard their door shut and realized I'd been holding my breath. Their voices were indistinct and after they'd shut the door I could only distinguish the fact the Pappa was speaking but I could only hear the muffled tones. He seemed to go on and on. I could only barely make out an occasional murmur from my Mamma.

My terror was complete almost to the point of hysteria when I heard their door open and both of them go downstairs. Jana wasn't back and I was really scared.

Now that Pappa was home I'd have to remain upstairs. I am actually glad he doesn't want to see me for I don't think I could bear to see his extreme anger.

The baby is very active today. It's as though it wants to be out so it can run away. I believe it picks up my feelings. It must know I'm planning to escape as soon as I can get it arranged with David.

I could lay in bed no longer. The baby thrashed around and my back hurt dreadfully. I moved to sit in the window seat before the window. We stored blankets there and underneath the blankets was a loose board that when lifted opened into the space between the two floors of the house. I now kept my diary hidden on a small ledge under the loose board. I told Jana where it was hidden. I now shared everything with her.

I looked out over the bay. It glimmered in the moonlight. I had looked out the window often and for long periods of time this day. The water that now was only a silvery sheen in the moonlight had sparkled and tossed with so much life. The greenery shimmered like emeralds and the little blue butterflies of

which I was so fond, frolicked around the hill
top. Birds sang their little hearts out in
gratitude of their freedom there in their
sunlit paradise. I thought of how I'd love to
be able to join them in their freedom. How I'd
love to be free to walk along the beach with
David.

I daydreamed of these things as I waited for
Jana's return.

I began to hear a lot of noise, the sounds
filtering up the stairway and through the
closed door of our room. My heart lurched when
I realized the noise I heard was hammering. I
thought of the sound of David doing carpenter
work. It brought tears of nostalgia to my
eyes. Those days had been so beautiful. A
thought crossed my mind, paralyzing me with
it's dreadfulness.

Could Pappa have lured David over with the
promise of a job—or to talk—so some of his
seamen or he himself could beat him? Pappa was
a huge man with great strength.

I opened my door so I could listen for any
cry for help. I knew I'd rush downstairs to
help David if it were him. I'd beg for his
life. I'd promise them anything they wanted
and still wait my chance to get away.

I drew back from the doorway and flung
myself into bed by the blanket form that I
hoped would represent Jana should anyone look
in. I had heard swift footsteps on the stairs.
My heart was beating in a frenzy.

Jana rushed inside our room. "We're being
made prisoners!" she gasped. She looked at the
blanket form in the bed and sort of smiled.

"So who do you have there?" she asked.

"You," I said and smiled as well as I could.
We quickly returned the blankets to the window

box. Jana was explaining in whispers as she worked.

She said she had almost not made it back inside in time. She said Pappa was fixing locks on all the doors and nailing the windows shut. He'd started on the garden room door right after Jana had slipped inside.

"I would have been trapped outside in a matter of moments!" she'd exclaimed.

"Has he gone mad?" I had asked.

"Disgrace doesn't sit well with him, that's for certain," Jana replied. "I don't know whether he's locking us in or David out; both, I guess."

At the mention of David's name my heart gave a wrench. "Oh! No!" I thought, "If he didn't get the letter I'd sent by Jana then I'd lost all possibility of contact with him." Jana saw my stricken look and said, "David came up as I was leaving the letter under a stone. I told him what has been happening. He was very upset. He said to tell you that you can live with him, his aunt and his uncle. You can marry immediately and legally. He wants you and the baby and wants you to somehow escape now. He will wait by the dunes every night and he will be careful that no one discovers him there."

"He won't know we're nailed and locked in," I said, feeling more desperate than ever. "I'll have to get another letter to him. I'll write it and if you find the chance, take it quickly to the dunes tomorrow and leave it for him, will you, Jana?" I pleaded.

"You know I will," Jana agreed, "but this frightens me more each day."

\*\*\*\*\*\*

I've hidden some of my writing paper and a
tiny bottle of ink and some quills under the
window box with my diary. I am afraid all
sources of contact with David will be cut off.

I've talked to Jana again about my hiding
place for you, dear diary. I've reminded her
that you are a record of my love and that no
matter where I go, it will always be there. We
have been concerned that mice might be under
the floors and chew on you, so Jana has looked
around and found a small metal safe box to fit
you into. It's iron and quite strong with a
lock built into it and a tiny key to fit the
lock. Pappa brought it back from one of his
voyages. We had seen it stowed away when we
were bringing books down from the attic.

Jana sneaked it from the attic and handed it
to me. It was perfect for the few things I
wanted to safe keep.

I resent being imprisoned. Jana has checked
all the windows and said they are all nailed
firmly shut. The doors have big locks on them.
Our window hasn't been nailed shut for it is
quite high and there's nothing below but a
sheer fall.

Jana said all the other windows have been
nailed shut, even the ones in Mamma and
Pappa's room. She checks them as she helps
with the housework when Mamma isn't around.
The doors are unlocked when Pappa leaves, but
Mamma is on watch until he comes home. The
only reason our window hasn't been nailed
shut, I think, is because Pappa can't face me.
It's a sad blessing.

Jana has convinced our parents that she knew
nothing of me and David. They think he seduced
me as he built the garden room and ruined me
the day Mamma went to the mainland, leaving me
there and taking Jana with her.

Jana and I do nothing to dispel this theory. It's good that Mamma doesn't remember the exact date or isn't thinking of it for it was well after that, that David and I became intimate. I'd have had our baby by then had that been the case. I think she has a lot on her mind and is grabbing at straws.

I'm glad I didn't go into any real detail when I confessed my love for David to her. I'm glad I didn't speak of any of the past events and only of the present set of events when I'd written to David and had the letter snatched by Pappa. This way Jana can remain above suspicion we hope.

They think Jana is watching me for them. She's doing all she can, though, to keep me free and save my baby.

**\* \* \* \* \* \***

I don't know why I did it, but I felt compelled to leave a mark of my love for David on the house I would soon be leaving, either as a captive of my parents or as a fugitive fleeing for my life and the life of our baby. Yesterday I took a small knife from the kitchen. I sat midway up the stairs pretending to read. While there I was actually carving a message on the stair rail. I carved out, quite deeply, 'Janis and David—forever'. I carefully swept up the shavings into my handkerchief.

Jana came to sit beside me and when she saw it she said, "Janis, don't you know that will only provoke Pappa further? If you ever expect to get free you must appear meek."

She got the beeswax and pretended to be waxing the stair rail. It was beautiful, made of mahogany and an item that Pappa had shipped from an island when the house was being built.

Jana mixed some bootblack and vermilion color with the wax to match the color of the rail. She worked hard to pack the carving full of the mixture and to blend it into the natural color of the railing. When she finished, it couldn't be noticed unless one knew where to look.

I explained to Jana how I felt about leaving a mark on the house.

She understood, but said, "But couldn't it have been made somewhere that Pappa wouldn't notice."

I said, "Too many things are being hidden." I was making plans to escape just before we sailed. I would wait for as long as I dared but I knew it would have to be soon. I had asked David to provide Jana with a strong rope so I could climb from our window. It was behind the house under some canvas bags filled with fishing gear and nets. Some tools were under the small lean-to with the bags and a few other odds and ends.

Jana said David had tied loops so I could work my way down safely. We were going to tie one end of the rope to the bedpost and after I had escaped, Jana would untie it and throw it down to us.

In case we lost the ability to pass letters, we'd put a red scarf from our window on the day we were to set me free. The plan was that on that day after everyone was asleep I'd climb down.

Without Jana I'd go mad. God blessed me with my twin.

****** 

Last night Jana seemed troubled. I had to force her to tell me what was wrong.

185

"You have so many troubles already," she said.

I kept insisting and she said, "Pappa has told me that Jared Winslow has asked his permission to court me. Pappa has told him perhaps after Mamma has given us our 'European tour', but that soon after that we're to go to Philadelphia to finishing school.

"Jared will be attending an eastern college and Pappa has given his permission for the courtship."

"I'm sorry you will have to go through this first," I said.

"I wish I could go away, and Jared, too," Jana said. "At least we know there'll be no 'European tour'," I said. "How like Pappa to describe it that way! He can be so pompous!" Now Jana is learning about love.

\*\*\*\*\*\*

Two things happened today. Pappa has arranged passage. We're to leave in four days.

The other thing is that I've been having some pains. Jana is trying to get out of the house to tell David I'll be ready to escape tomorrow night after everyone is asleep.

David plans to hide me with some Indian friends who live in the swamps. They would never think to look for me there. He knows that as soon as I am discovered to be missing that Pappa will come after him. His aunt will deliver the baby and they know a preacher who will marry us because I'm pregnant and so the baby will have it's rightful father.

I can't wait! We have selected clothing I'll need and a few personal things. We've packed them in a valise that Jana got down from the attic on the pretense of using it for the trip. She also found the christening dress I'd worn as a baby. It is still beautiful. The satin is yellowed to ivory and the overlay of lace is so lovely. It has a cute matching bonnet. Our little baby rings were there and she brought mine to me.

I know that I will desperately miss my sister but I thank God she will have Jared to comfort her.

We've hidden the valise under the bed. After I've escaped, Jana will drop the valise. I'm happy and I'm scared and I'm dreaming of my life with David.

******

Jana managed to get the letter out to the dunes this morning while Mamma was finishing some of her sewing. I'm writing this early because I may not be able to write more tonight. I will pack you, dear diary, in my valise tonight as well as a few other things I've gathered up.

I'll probably never see Pappa again.

Jana said she'll find a way to contact me.

I don't know what Mamma will do and it breaks my heart. I know that I'd rather die than to live the life they have chosen for me. David is my soul.

My baby lies low in my belly and I know it won't be long. The pains are still there.

******

How naive I was when I last wrote in you, dear diary. The night that I was to leave with David didn't happen. I began to have more frequent pains after breakfast, but they came and went. I was sleepy all day and stayed in bed a lot for I knew I'd need all the rest I could get for what I expected to face that night.

By mid-afternoon I began to cramp off and on. I lay back down, for I'd gone downstairs to get a couple of books I'd decided to take with me. Jana rubbed my back with some soothing ointment.

After dinner, which Jana brought up to me, the pain got so much worse. By nine o'clock I was in agony. I let Jana get Mamma. I had been trying to wait until everyone went to sleep so I could climb down the rope that Jana had smuggled upstairs to our room.

I was doubled over with pain which had become constant. When something warm and wet gushed from between my legs soaking the bed I thought I was bleeding to death. Jana and I looked and decided I'd urinated. I tried to get up so we could change the bed, but collapsed in pain instead. It was then that I let Jana call Mamma.

Mamma rushed in and looked at me. She and Jana helped me onto the bed and Mamma began to cry. I had held back my cries, afraid I'd alert Mamma and Pappa and wouldn't be able to escape. The next few pains made me scream in agony. I could see Jana's frightened face. I was terrified.

I saw Mamma's hand as though it floated toward me. She patted my face as another pain tore through my body. Mamma ran from the room and Jana raised me up to hold me close. We were both crying. We heard Mamma shout to Pappa, "Her baby is coming!" Everyone was talking at once. I heard Pappa swear. I cringed at the sound. Pains tore me apart. I thought I was dying and I tried to pray. All I could think of was David.

Jana was sent to boil water. Pappa was sent to find sheets and some flannel in Mamma's sewing room. I was only dimly aware of this. I felt myself rolled around as the bed was being fixed and my clothing removed. Mamma and Jana held my hands on each side and I heard Mamma saying, "Push out the baby, Janis!" She seemed to be saying it over and over.

I heard it through my screams. "Push, Janis—PUSH! PUSH! As hard as you can!" I heard and felt her lean over and put a kiss on my forehead. I think Mamma's kiss gave me courage to push harder than ever. Now Mamma seemed to be holding my legs open and Jana squeezed my hand—or I was squeezing hers.

I was so filled with fear and pain that I wavered between consciousness and unconsciousness. My heart was joyous when I heard a tiny cry and then a lustier one.

"It's a boy!" I heard Mamma say. The pain was awful again. The relief had been so brief. I heard myself scream louder than I'd screamed yet. I couldn't stop.

Suddenly it was over and I heard Mamma say something about 'another one'. I heard the baby crying and someone, I think Jana, said, "It's a girl". I was certain it had been a boy.

I fell asleep. I woke once and David was beside me. Jana had let him up the rope. David had been below. He could hear the screams and was about to tear down the door when Jana had gone to the window and made a rocking motion of her arms. She signaled him to wait. When she felt it was safe she had let down the rope. She whispered to us both.

We had twins—a boy and a girl. David kissed me. His eyes glowed with happiness.

"When I can get up and get out with the babies I'll come," I promised.

"I'm going to ask your Pappa for your hand in marriage," David said. "I will do it tomorrow morning." "Surely he will now," I said. We thought we heard a sound.

Jana whispered, "You'd better go. Hurry!"

David stepped over the window box and disappeared from sight. I lay back and slept, feeling happier than I'd felt in months. "Surely he will," I thought as I fell asleep. David hadn't been able to see our babies and neither had I, for Mamma had taken them away after placing them at my breast. Jana said they suckled while I slept.

**\* \* \* \* \* \***

`I awoke to Pappa's loud roar. He was yelling at someone downstairs. I listened and thought I could hear David's soft voice obviously trying to reason with him.

I tried to get up but Jana pushed me back onto my pillow. I felt too weak to resist. My struggle was feeble. "You can't get up," she said. "You bled a lot and Mamma said it was much more than normal. She said you are not to stand up or move around. You may hemorrhage to death. You've got to stay well, Janis so you can escape with your babies if Pappa won't let you marry David."

I heard a tiny cry and Mamma came in with two babies. They were so tiny and so funny looking. I loved them instantly. I reached out my arms.

"They're beautiful!" I said. Mamma placed them in my arms.

"They're hungry. Here I'll help you," she said, unbuttoning my shift and placing the babies to my breast. I had never thought so far as to nursing my baby while I was pregnant. I was delighted. Soon I had two tiny mouths pulling at my enlarged breasts. There was a soreness in my breasts but such a feeling of joy as the babies nursed. "Which is which?" I asked proudly. I was pointed out the boy and then the girl.

"I'll name the girl Jana after my sister and the boy David after his father. Their last name will be David's and if that is Pappa yelling at David he mustn't for I am going to marry him!"

"Your Pappa will never allow it," Mamma said. My heart sank. The babies stirred at my breast and one of them gave a little mewing cry. I settled them closer to my breast and they suckled on.

"Even now?" I asked Mamma in amazement. "I can't believe that, Mamma!"

"He still plans to send us off to Europe and he wants you to adopt out the babies. He says he WILL NOT have Jana's chance for a good marriage ruined because our family is in disgrace. He will not allow you to marry beneath you, ruined or not. He will cover up your disgrace, and we will go on as before."

"Mamma! How can you let him do this?" I cried out.

"I can't stop him, child," she said.

My precious babies suckled through this horrible revelation.

After Mamma took the babies away Jana and I talked. "I'll help you," she said, hugging me tight. She got a brush and gently brushed out my tangled mass of hair. She poured water into the basin from the ewer by the bed and washed my face with a soft cloth.

"I'll bring a large basin up and help you with the rest of your bath," she said.

We heard a door slam loudly downstairs and right after that Pappa's footsteps pounded up the stairs. Jana and I froze. We stared at each other in fear. I pulled the covers over my babies and waited. He continued on down the hallway to his and Mamma's room.

Their door closed but we could hear him talking loudly. We couldn't hear Mamma. Soon he pounded back down the stairs and we heard the front door close though not so loudly as before.

"I think he is gone," Jana said in a whisper. I sank weakly into the pillows.

"I will marry David," I told Jana. "We are married in God's sight—and we will be married by a priest or preacher in the eyes of man, so that our babies won't be called bastards."

I slept, nursed the babies and managed to eat a little bread and some broth.

Once when I woke up Jana said I was bleeding too much and Mamma had gone to the mainland to the apothecary to buy some herbs so she could brew some tea to stop my bleeding.

I asked if she'd take a letter to David for me. She brought me paper, pen and ink and I hurriedly wrote to him, assuring him that as soon as I was strong enough I would escape with our babies.

I told him that the night when I was able to go there would be a red scarf in the window that day. I also told him our babies names were Jana and David. I told him how beautiful they were, and how happy I was with them. I also told him of Pappa's plans.

Jana took the letter to the dunes. "Soon I'll be with David," I told her and lay sleeping with our babies.

192

\* \* \* \* \* \*

Mamma brought in some sort of nursing bottles for the babies. They were glass and held a teat-looking cap for the babies to suck. I have had fever for several days and she thought it wasn't good to feed the babies fevered milk. I have to squeeze out my milk and my breasts hurt.

I missed nursing my babies. I loved to hold them close and feel their little mouths taking nourishment from my body.

Mamma began to leave the babies in her room and I'd have to ask to see them. Jana said she thought Mamma was trying to wean me from the babies.

That frightened me because I had to have my babies near me when I became able to flee with them. I could hardly expect to sneak them out of Mamma and Pappa's room during the night.

I wouldn't speak to Mamma after she started keeping my babies from me. Finally Mamma returned my babies. They were crying at night and keeping Pappa awake.

"They were crying for me," I told her.

My fever has gone and I feel a little stronger. The bleeding is much less. With the babies now sleeping in our room Jana and I had learned how to care for them.

I dared not wait much longer. I told Jana I was ready to flee with my babies. That it was time to notify David.

Jana thought I should wait a little longer until the babies crying and us moving up and down the stairs to get their milk was an established routine.

I started moving around the house and my fever came back. The bleeding increased and Mamma gave me the tea again and made special broths to strengthen me. I realized I was still too weak to be able to run with David and the babies. I daydreamed constantly of the day when we could all be together.

\*\*\*\*\*\*

Jana said Pappa is frantic to get us off to Europe. When we go, she told me, we will be leaving by carriage to another port where we'll be booked for passage to Europe.

No one will know us there to report us leaving with two mysterious babies. Jana and I alone draw enough attention.

Jana has been warned not to let me know. We are to be leaving within a week. I'll put out the red scarf tomorrow. Tonight we are adding baby things to the valise. Jana has brought me a couple of letters from David. He's so proud of our babies.

\*\*\*\*\*\*

I've not been able to write until today. I'm not sure how many days have passed. I've been ill and I still am. If it weren't for my tiny Jana and my hopes of finding little David I'm sure I'd die.

I still plan to flee this house. I will start at the beginning, dear diary, though I am so weary. Just the act of writing fatigues me sorely.

I put the red scarf in the window for David, just as planned. Jana had taken the front door key shortly after our parents went to bed. Waiting for hours to be sure Pappa was at his soundest sleep was agonizing.

We had lowered the valise on the rope after the lock was unlocked. David was to meet us beside the house where we used to meet to kiss. Jana was to take one baby and I'd take the other. We were careful not to wake the sleeping babies as we lifted them gently and drew their little quilts about them. Jana took baby David and I took little Jana.

My heart beat wildly as we descended the stairs. They seemed to creak louder than usual. Little Jana began to cry and my sister and I abandoned all caution as we rushed for the door. Jana was ahead of me.

David must have heard us, for he had just leaped onto the front porch as Jana burst through the doorway. She shoved baby David into his arms. He held the large valise in the other.

Suddenly Pappa was there. He grabbed my arm and I screamed for David to run with our son. I begged him to. My screams were wild with desperation.

"Save our son David!" I screamed. "Run! Run for his life!" David dropped the valise and ran.

Pappa released my arm to pursue David who had already disappeared among the dunes.

I tried to run with baby Jana but Pappa grabbed me again. He made Jana take my baby girl and he dragged me along behind her. Jana had no choice but to return to our room.

I fought frantically to get free. I even bit Pappa's hand as hard as I could. He raised his fist as though to strike me then lowered it as Mamma shouted out "no!". I was steeled for the blow for he intended to do it. I could see how frightened Mamma was.

While Mamma tried to quiet Jana, the crying baby and me, for all three of us were sobbing hysterically, we could hear Pappa beginning to hammer outside our door. When he came inside his face was as dark as a thunder cloud.

I sprang upon his back when he began to nail the window closed. I beat him with my fist as he had intended to beat me. I screamed and begged him to let me go to David and our son. Mamma pulled me off Pappa, and he nailed on without a word.

When he finished, he told Mamma to come with him. She hesitated only briefly, opened her mouth to protest, then followed him out of our room. Jana and I heard a lock click and footsteps walked away.

I was bleeding a lot and Jana beat on the door to tell Mamma. We heard voices and eventually Mamma brought up light snacks for Jana and me, and milk for the baby bottle that was still used during the times when I had fever. She went back down after locking the door behind her and brought up a pot of steaming tea to help stop my bleeding. She also had warm water and some fresh flannel for pads.

Pappa stood outside the door. I suppose he thought we might attack Mamma and run away. We could hear his harsh breaths as his anger escaped from him in gusts. Mamma left us begging her to set us free. Pappa locked the door again.

The next day Jana was moved to another room. She and I had shared a room and a bed since we were born. The absence of Jana and of my baby boy made me feel as though parts of me had been torn away.

My little girl is my solace and I live in fear that they will come in and tear her away from me.

I look out the window constantly. I sit there holding my little girl each day, and at night I often sleep there hoping I will hear David outside.

Jana gets to visit me a few hours each day. My fever is much worse and I am often bathed with cool cloths and given awful tasting things to drink. Mamma comes in to clean the room, remove the baby wraps and to empty the chamber pot.

Snacks and water are left for me. Books are stacked should I care to read, but there is no way I could read. My meals are brought up and I notice my favorite foods are fixed for me.

Food revolts me and I've begun vomiting. Sometimes Mamma tries to hold me in her arms and I push her away. I know I would never allow anyone to hurt my children as she is allowing us to be hurt.

Jana is devastated. She tells me that neither David nor the baby can be found. Pappa has some of his roughest seamen combing the island for David. No one, of course, mentions the baby, for Pappa is determined to keep the babies a secret so he can get rid of them like a bunch of stray cats.

I am so sadly disappointed in my parents. I'll never let Mamma hug me again. Pappa is a stranger to me—a cruel and selfish stranger that I abhor. My world where I had loving parents ended. I feel that it never existed for the strangers who hold us prisoners aren't the parents I knew. It's as though they died and someone looking like them stepped into our home.

All I think about is getting my baby out of here and finding David and our little son.

I've wearied myself too much. I look out the window for David as I write. The little blue butterflies are dancing above the hilltop and the birds still sing. Their worlds have been left undisturbed. They are free and can fly.

******

Jana said Mamma is trying to get Pappa to bring a doctor in to see me. I am often delirious, Jana said. She stays in my room now to help with the baby. She can go in and out when she knocks loud enough to be heard.

We're both prisoners. Jana by choice more or less and myself through a horrible set of social mores that have allowed the creation of evil such as this.

I believe Pappa is insane. Maybe he's always been. Maybe I just tipped the scales. If I caused his insanity I am deeply remorseful, but I feel hatred for him and that hatred spills over to Mamma. Her weakness is destroying the happiness of her children and her grandchildren.

How dare they use me and my children so callously and call it 'saving face'!

I thought I saw David during one of my bouts with delirium. Jana had to restrain me to keep me from throwing myself through the window.

I have decided that if David comes I will beat out the glass and toss little Jana to him. I will then jump from the window, for there will be no time to use the rope and go down slowly. I thought it out and that is my plan. There is no other way out. The minute they hear breaking glass they'll be in.

******

A new plan has been hatched. Jana heard Mamma sobbing her heart out and she pressed her ear to the door.

Mamma was pleading for Pappa to send Jana, little Jana, and me to Iowa. She will say that little Jana is her child—one of those 'change of life' babies. She's threatened to leave Pappa if he doesn't agree.

"Pappa is furious," Jana said.

"How can she think I'd give my little Jana to her?" I asked.

"Listen to me," Jana explained. "It's a way out. Once you get to Iowa, you can find a way to run with the baby. If Mamma can do it—if she can force Pappa—act as though it's a good plan. Act GRATEFUL.

I never thought that Mamma would have the nerve to oppose Pappa. I was beginning to think she didn't care for us, that she was as heartless as Pappa has been. You should have heard her sobbing, Janis. Her heart was broken." Jana and I clung together.

"You're right," I said to her. "It's our way out." After that I slept a real sleep for the first time in a long time. My nights and days had been ones of wild dreams and delirious fantasies. The fever and strong teas kept me in a state of confusion.

\*\*\*\*\*\*

Mamma spoke with us today. Pappa has agreed to an extended visit to Iowa for us. It will be told that Mamma's health hasn't been good since the birth of the baby and that we've come there to escape the mosquitoes and the sultry weather. She'll say the late life baby has left her with weakness and a shortness of breath.

I asked, "But how can I leave my other baby?"

"This is your only way to save your little girl," Mamma said. Tears ran down my face as I agreed.

Jana sneaked out one last letter for David. I'd heard nothing since he'd run with our baby.

**\* \* \* \* \* \***

Tomorrow we're to leave. I've had a red scarf in the window for two days. I sit on the window seat constantly, even fall asleep there some nights. When I'm not there Jana watches for me so I can rest on the bed. We take turns as we can. I'll watch for him all night tonight. If he comes I'll escape this time.

I've used a small orange stick to remove as much putty from around the window panes as I can do safely. A small tap on each pane will cause them to fall. I've devised a sling from a coverlet to let the baby down in. We've decided not to pack a valise. I'll try to slide down the rope after the baby is safely in David's arms. Jana will help me.

This is my last chance. I pray that David will see the scarf in time.

Jana will keep you, dear diary, and return you to me when we next meet. I am sure that without the baby and me there will be no need to go to Iowa.

David and I will hide out with our babies until after we are legally married.

I pray he has seen the red scarf for night is about to fall. A partial moon will be out lighting the island only dimly. We'll be swallowed up by shadows if we get a small lead.

We've devised a sugar teat for little Jana should she begin to cry. She loves to suck on the teat. I can take no chances of discovery.

**✶ ✶ ✶ ✶ ✶ ✶**

So many things have happened. I'll try to set it all down and return this diary to Janis as I promised to do. This too will be my last chance—to see my sister and to return her diary and the few precious things she'd placed in the box with it. Janis is in the parlor and baby Jana is with Mamma.

Tomorrow we leave for Iowa—Mamma, little Jana and me. I've cried until I'm dry. My heart is a stone. I'm lost in a gulf of darkness. A part of me is dead for my precious sister is dead.

To continue this diary for Janis is so hard. The night she planned to escape had been nerve wracking. We peered out the window and listened to every sound.

It was late when Janis whispered, "I think I hear someone outside!" We pressed our faces against the glass window pane.

Suddenly there was a loud thump just as a cloud cleared the moon.

Someone lifted a large object and struck someone else. The person who was struck fell and both were lost in shadows.

Someone ran and a loud knocking sound erupted at the front door. We heard Pappa running downstairs. Footsteps ran to beneath our window. Janis and I strained to see through the shadows.

We heard sounds as though something heavy were being dragged across the yard. We were terrified. It seemed only a short time later that we saw forms on the hill. Someone, or two people, were digging at the sand—and vine-covered knoll.

Things were happening so fast. We could hear underbrush breaking and the shovel striking a stone occasionally with a clang as clear as a bell.

Janis was out of her mind with fear. She wanted to push out the window, lower the baby and run with it.

As we watched the clouds scuttled past the moon. The scene on the hilltop was one of horror. Two men had just lifted another man and as we watched he was dropped into the hole they'd dug.

Janis screamed, "Pappa! Pappa has killed David!" and she leaped from the window taking all of the loosened panes with her.

I leaned from the window, calling her name. There was no answer. The sound of the breaking glass lingered in my ears.

The men on the hillside ran. There was the sound of rushing feet coming toward our window. I withdrew my head but not before I saw Pappa and a large rough-looking man beside him.

I hoped Janis had run. I heard low voices and then the voices went away. I thought I heard someone sobbing.

Pappa's footsteps came up the stairs and after awhile Mamma screamed.

I was afraid Pappa had struck her because Janis had escaped. I beat on the door frantically for we'd been securely locked in all this time.

Mamma opened the door. Her face was as white a chalk in the candlelight. I heard Pappa going back downstairs. Mamma finally told me that Janis broke her neck when she jumped from the window. A piece of glass had pierced her heart.

There's a huge pile of sand under my window to cover and to soak up her blood.

I watched out the window as Pappa covered up the hole where I'm sure they had thrown David, without benefit of coffin or a decent burial. Then he began to dig another one. This one for Janis.

Tomorrow Janis will be buried. She is in her coffin in the parlor. She wears her blue dress Mamma had ordered for her travel in. It's too big for her now but that doesn't show. She looks so sweet and peaceful there—just as though she sleeps.

I know that part of me will be buried with her. I'll put this diary beneath her skirts tonight.

After a private funeral tomorrow, we will leave for Iowa. We will say Janis died of the fever. That will make it seem even more important for Mamma to leave the mosquito infestation of the island—or so we'll say.

I never want to see Pappa again. I don't think Mamma loves him anymore either.

* * * * * *

The diary ended. Janna and David sat there looking at each other. Janna tried to stand and cried out. Every muscle in her body ached. The scrapes and scratches burned and her mind raced at the speed of light. David caught her arm or she would have fallen.

"Someone is going to bed and I'm bringing her a bowl of hot soup and something soothing to drink. You're as hoarse as a frog and in agony, honey."

"I had to know," Janna practically croaked. She'd been reading for an eternity—Janis and David's eternity.

They went up to the room where the diary had been written day by heartbreaking day. David helped her as they went up the stairs. They paused mid-way and both of their hands lovingly touched the pledge of love between David and Janis.

"Forever," Janna said and David kissed her saying, "Yes, forever."

They entered the room with a feeling of reverence. So much had happened from this room. They now knew that they had nothing to fear from the room. It was where they belonged.

David helped Janna on with a soft flannel gown and pulled back the covers, lifting her onto the tall four poster.

"I think we're going to have to research some family history," Janna said, "but certainly not tonight."

"I'm thinking some pretty crazy thoughts," David said. "Me, too," Janna replied. As Janna and David slept in the big bed in the room upstairs another couple stood hand in hand watching them.

"I wonder what they'll name the twins?" a ghostly whisper murmured.

"Janis and David," of course, she answered with a soft laugh...and finally they could rest in peace.

# THE HURRICANE

The hurricane that was to have gone to land miles away had suddenly turned from the mainland where it was to have hit and stalled over the gulf. It seethed there gaining in fury.

Janna and David decided to pack just in case.

"We can't take chances with the babies due in three weeks," David had said, leaning over to kiss Janna's protruding stomach.

"They've dropped this week—see how low they are riding now?" Janna asked pushing her stomach out proudly. "And you know what they say about first babies—they can come early or late."

"I can't wait to see them, Janna," David said.

"Neither can I," she answered rubbing her hands over her stomach where she'd just been kicked from within. They continued to pack Janna's small car. The top was up on the car and they had it crammed with things they'd bought for the babies, and the few things they'd packed for themselves.

David unplugged the clock radio and stuffed it in between some pillows and blankets they'd brought along. They had decided to travel inland to Atlanta and stay there until after the babies were born.

The winds had increased steadily as they packed the car. David bad begun to hurry Janna. They heard sirens shrieking as they started out the door with their sleeping bags, a cooler of food and drinks and the two little dogs. The sirens shrieking joined the howling of the wind. The dogs fought to get free.

"Take the dogs and get in the bathroom!" David said. "I'll get the battery radio from the closet." He shoved a protesting Janna into the small downstairs bath which had probably been built as a large pantry off the kitchen. He tossed the sleeping bags and the cooler in after her and the dogs.

Janna stood in the doorway of the bath terrified to be separated from him. She heard his footsteps pound up the stairs, then get lost in the sound of wind and wailing sirens.

A sharp pain gripped her stomach and she sank to the floor. She clutched her stomach, expecting another that didn't come. "Gas," she said.

David came running back down the stairs. He saw Janna sitting on the floor just inside the door. "Honey, take the sleeping bags and sit on them," he said as he moved the knobs on the radio to get a rash of ugly sounds and loud static.

Finally a garbled voice came over the radio. They listened breathlessly. David leaned his ear close to the radio. He listened for awhile then turned toward Janna. His face was drained of color. His freckles no longer blended with his tan.

Another pain tore through Janna's body. She gave a small cry and clutched her stomach. Her little dogs pressed close to her. She heard David speaking through her pain. The wind howled and she thought she could still hear sirens. Something warm gushed from between her legs and she knew her water had broken. Her terror became acute.

"David we've got to get to the hospital! I think the babies are coming!" she cried out.

David stood staring at her with his mouth open. Their eyes met and she was sure she saw fear tear across his face.

"Honey, we CAN'T," he said. "The causeway is flooded and a portion of it is washed away. The hurricane changed course and has created huge waves. It's headed for the island."

The third pain tore at Janna's stomach. She gasped for breath. "Stay here!" David said. "I'll be right back!"

Jana was terrified as she watched him run from the room. She rose to follow and fell back to her knees. She doubled over holding her stomach. She remembered something about timing her pains. She looked at her watch. Three minutes later she cried out aloud. Sweat had broken out on her body and it ran down her face and into her eyes where it joined her tears. She knew she was going into labor.

David rushed back in. His arms were filled with items which he tossed in the door. Before she could tell him she was in labor he was gone again. She began to cry loudly. The next pain came as David came in and slammed the door behind him.

"David! I'm in labor!" she gasped out. He kissed her quickly and wiped her face with a hand towel.

"I thought you might be," he said. He began to spread bedding in the bottom of the big old bath tub. First he put in a thick padding of large pillows. Then he folded a thick down coverlet over that and some old quilts. He tore down the shower curtain and tucked it over the soft bed he'd made. He folded a thick flannel blanket on top of the plastic shower curtain.

As Janna watched the next pain seemed to come quicker. She had forgotten to keep time.

"Let's take off your jeans," David said and lifted her onto his lap as he sat on the commode and worked her maternity jeans down her hips. They were wet, and smelled of a strange odor.

"My water," she said as another pain stabbed her. David held her close.

"Honey, we're going to put you into the tub. It's the best I can do," David said. "Just remember the manger—at least it's not in a barn out in the cold somewhere!"

Jana tried to smile. Her face was dripping sweat again and the pains were almost a comfort. She tried to stifle back the cries but they came from her lips of their own violation.

David helped her into the tub. He put a pillow under her head and raised her legs to the rim of the tub on each side.

"Now, keep your feet up here and push with the pains," he instructed. "Just remember, when this is over we will have our beautiful babies. I'd give anything to take this pain from you, my precious one," he said. She could hear the anguish in his voice.

She and David had read childbirth books together and had been eagerly awaiting the birth of their babies. They'd laughed at the possibility of the babies being born in the car as David sped off to the hospital. It was a joke then. Never could they have they imagined the situation they'd actually find themselves in. They were prepared academically—but not for this.

Janna screamed and pushed. David tried to coach her breathing. He leaned over her, holding her hands as she gripped his strong, rough hands and pushed. He let her hands go occasionally between the worst pains.

At one point she was aware of a strong smell of alcohol and the sound of something metal being dropped into the wash basin. The alcohol smell in the close bathroom atmosphere was nauseating. Just as she thought she'd vomit, a savage pain tore through her body. She felt David's hand press her shoulders.

"Push with your feet! PUSH, JANNA, PUSH!" he was yelling. She felt the baby tear itself from her body and was dimly aware that David reached between her legs. She tried desperately to hold on to consciousness.

A little cry reached her ears as another flash of agony seemed to tear her limb from limb.

Something wet seemed to fall on her chest. As she reached to push it away it let out a cry. "My baby!" she thought as her hand fell weakly to find its way to a warm, wet little body.

Another cry joined the cries of the baby on her chest and Janna lost consciousness.

Janna seemed to waver between being asleep and being awake. She was conscious of David doing things to her. She'd sometimes hear babies cry. Once she'd heard David scold Muffy and Puffy. "No, they're not toys!" she seemed to be saying. "Of course my dogs aren't toys," she thought and dozed back off to sleep.

Throughout it all, Janna had seen them—had known they were there. They'd stood behind David as he helped her bring her babies into the world. She hadn't seen them since she and David had finished the diary—over eight months ago. She thought they had gone and somehow she had missed them.

Sometimes she knew that David left the room. It seemed strange to be bedded in the bathtub. The babies were somewhere beside her when

David took them from her breast after they nursed. When they cried she knew David would place them to her breast. Their little cries would stop and little mouths would pull at her full breasts, bringing little thrills of delight to her whole body. Her hands would pass over them.

Little Janis and David were so sweet. David fed and nursed Janna. He bathed her and helped her with a bed pan of sorts that he'd contrived from a roaster cover. Janna had no concept of time.

When she was finally able to stay awake David told her what had happened.

The hurricane had gone across the opposite end of the island. A tree had fallen and crushed her car. David had rescued most of their possessions from the car after the winds had died down somewhat.

The bridge was still not navigable. They were trapped on the island. He hadn't wanted to leave her to find out what had happened to the other people who'd been stranded on the island.

David asked her, "Do you think you're ready for a real bed yet?"

"I long for it," she answered.

Janna laughed, "I'll never see a nativity scene again without remembering this!"

"Could we stay in our room upstairs?" Janna asked.

"I'll carry you up the stairs," David said. "I want our babies to stay there in the room with us both the way they should have done those years ago."

David looked at her. "Did you see them, too?" he asked.

"Yes," she answered," they were there all the time."

"I know," David said.

****** 

The winds still howled but not with the fierceness that it had during the three days it had teased the coastline and the island.

Another hurricane had been building and seemed to be traveling the same pathway. It was expected to hit miles down the coast.

David helped Janna upstairs. He carried her and then went down for the babies.

The large four poster was heavenly after the days spent in the bathtub. Janna's back was stiff and she seemed sore all over.

Janna smiled when she'd seen the bed David had made for the twins. It was a large wooden crate they'd found on the beach. It had bleached a beautiful silvery gray and had held sea food at one time. Filled with big pillows it made a perfect bed for the tiny babies.

The crib had been crushed when the tree fell on Janna's car. David lugged the box upstairs and the babies slept peacefully in their makeshift crib. Janna's little dogs seemed to have appointed themselves watchers of the babies. They lay beside the box and wouldn't go willingly to their own basket. Finally David moved their basket close to the babies box then they climbed in they curled around to get comfortable and wiggled their tails as they looked at Janna and David.

They laughed. "That's what they wanted!" Janna said. "They want to be near the babies!"

****** 

The next morning, David settled Janna and the babies in and left. He was walking down the beach to see what was happening on the island and to get some groceries. He wanted to buy baby bottles, diapers, and formula if he could find them. Too many trees had blown down for him to attempt to drive his big truck.

Janna listened to the radio. She slept and nursed the babies while he was away. She wanted to nurse the babies for awhile but she also wanted to have bottles and formula on hand. It would, also, be a sheer luxury to have disposable diapers.

The babies were so sweet. She thought she could see a combination of both her and David's features beginning to appear as their little eyes and faces became less puffy and the newborn redness cleared away. They seemed to be identical, other than being a little boy and girl.

She was half dozing as the babies nursed. Suddenly she realized what she was hearing on the radio. She'd swear the volume had been turned up. Janna's full attention was on the static-y voice coming from the radio.

The hurricane had turned—it was headed for the island. It was reported to have twice the force of Hurricane Travis that had just glanced off the tip of the island.

Janna moved the sleeping babies into their box. Her little dogs had gone out with David. She was cold with fear. She went to the window and looked out. Strange feelings assailed her as she looked out over the trees and vines to see the waves on the bay leaping high against their barrier of land. White spray flung itself from the crashing waves. The bay was usually so peaceful with it's ripples and playful little eddies. It was often like a wavy glass mirror—it's surface broken by diving pelicans, skimming oyster catchers, sea

gulls, or fish breaking the sparkling surface.
Sometimes little winds rippled it into gentle
lapping waves or passing boats and barges
rolled their turbulence shoreward. Nothing in
the bay's everyday life cycle pushed it into a
fury like this.

Janna fought a sudden and wild impulse to
grab her babies and leap from the window. A
sudden chill brought her back to reality. She
thought of the diary and knew whose fear she
was feeling in addition to her own.

She went over to look at her sleeping
babies. She kissed each dear little face. She
soon heard running footsteps on the stairs.

"Pack a few things for the babies. We can't
carry much. The military is sending a
helicopter for the people on the island.
People are being assigned numbers as they come
in. We have to hurry. Dress the babies warmly,
Janna. We can always take off their clothes if
they get too hot. I'll gather a few things for
us!" David was breathless.

He soon had them all downstairs. He held the
blanket-wrapped babies and their large diaper
bag. Janna carried the back pack on her back.
The little dogs had bounced in after David.
They rushed to the door with them.

"Oh! Lord! I forgot about them! They'll have
to stay." "But David," Janna protested, "we
can't just LEAVE them!"

"Sit here and hold the babies," David said
and rushed to the kitchen. He rushed into the
bathroom with a huge bag of dogfood, returning
to fill a large boiler of water. He grabbed a
stack of newspapers and lined the bathtub with
them. He quickly pulled an afghan from the
couch and put it down on the bathroom floor
for them. They had been following him back and

forth. He cuddled them quickly and put them on the afghan.

"We'll be back," he told them, pulling the door closed.

Janna was weak already.

"Hold to my arm," David said. "We've got to hurry." He cradled the babies close and they hurried along the small trail to the beach.

The waves crashed and roared. They came high upon the beach, and washed up great heaps of seaweed and debris. There was only a narrow portion of beach left around the base of the dunes. Often they had to wade through eddies that had scooped into the sand and ran back and forth like little rivers into the gulf. At one point they were forced to scramble over dunes to avoid the crashing waves. The wind was warm and damp and tore at them. It howled around them, whipping at their clothing and throwing sand into their eyes. It was like something alive with it's warm, soggy force.

It seemed an eternity before they reached the group of people standing beside the 'Watering Hole.' A large helicopter was rising off the small landing pad. People shielded their faces from the wind that threw stinging sand at them. Another helicopter was on the way they said.

Janna and David stumbled inside the 'Watering Hole' with the others who had missed the first flight off the island. As they came in, Janna noticed more people threading their way over the dunes and branches of downed trees that had blown across the street.

David found Janna a stool and helped her up on it. Everyone listened to the battery radio sitting on the bar. Joan waved at Janna from behind the bar. "Cute babies!" she called out.

Hoyt came over to help David hold the twins. They stood close by Janna. The island's first responders, civil defense and firemen were helping everyone they could reach. Everyone seemed to be working together.

The electricity had been out for several days. The owners of the 'Watering Hole' were passing out sandwiches of cold cuts, cheese and anything they could fix without heating it up.

Jay came in with his little girl. He held her close as he walked over to the radio and turned down the volume. There was absolute silence, except for the battering winds. Jay announced, "The first responders and firemen have just been notified by the civil defense that no more flights can be made to the island. The winds are too treacherous. The tug boats can't take off because the waves are sweeping over the decks. We'll do what we can to help, but we can't get anyone else off the island."

David pressed close to Janna. She felt tears stream down her face. "What can we do?" she asked.

David looked into her eyes. "I'm so sorry, Honey," he said.

"Our house has survived many of these hurricanes over the centuries," Janna said. "I wish we were back there."

"I don't feel safe here," David said, "but we can't get back along the beach. The water's too high now. A sudden wave could suck us out and you're still so weak, Janna."

Hoyt spoke up. "I'll help you with the babies. We'll go by the middle road. It's blocked by fallen trees and things the last damn hurricane left there, but the volunteers have been making some effort to clear it.

215

"The wind won't be so bad that way either, for it's protected on one side by the dunes. The blowing sand may be bad so you'll have to keep the babies faces covered. You'll need something over your face, Janna. Let's go," he said, taking charge.

Janna pulled three receiving blankets from the babies' diaper bag. Hoyt and David lightly covered the babies faces. Janna covered her face and reached for the backpack.

"Leave the backpack, honey," David said. "It's going to be a tough walk back." Hoyt walked ahead with baby David. Janna followed him and David followed her with little Janis. The wind ripped at them as soon as they opened the door. Hoyt kissed Joan and whispered to her.

"Doesn't she want to come with us?" Janna asked.

"She's afraid. I'll come back and stay with her," Hoyt said as he had walked out the door ahead of us.

"Stay between us, Janna," David said, bringing up the rear. The wind was cooler, wetter, and Janna thought it was louder than it had been when they had come in to the 'Watering Hole.'

She felt a wetness running down her legs and knew that her bleeding has increased. She slid her hand between her legs and saw bright blood on her fingers. She wiped them along the side of her jeans and hoped David didn't see the blood on her for he had enough to concern himself with as he fought along with Hoyt to save their babies.

Threading through broken branches over heaps of debris and over trunks of trees was exhaustive. Janna was glad David had brought her hiking boots to her. She was glad of the tough jeans and thick socks, even though her feet were wet. She sweated under her light windbreaker he'd had her wear over her long sleeved cotton shirt. The briars reached through the tough jeans and tore the windbreaker to shreds. She fought her way over the obstacles as fast as she could. She refused to slow them down. The safety of reaching their home pushed her on.

David and Hoyt wore their white rubber fisherman's boots. Sometimes they pulled or pushed her over an especially tough obstacle. She fought hard to make it on her own.

A huge piece of tin flashed past them. They all knew it could have sliced any of them like a blade. It had been close—too close. Pieces of wood joined the flying leaves and twigs as the hurricane came closer to the island.

Janna was blown down at one point and David pulled her to her feet with one hand as he clasped the baby to his chest with the other. Janna heard little David begin to cry and Hoyt talking to him.

When they approached, the house Janna fell on the steps. She heard David cry out, "Oh! God! She's bleeding!" She was close to fainting and barely hanging on.

Hoyt took the babies and went inside. They hadn't locked the big front door. Janna could hear one of the babies crying and the little dogs seemed to be screaming in fright. She felt David lift her into his arms and carry her inside. She heard David and Hoyt talking.

"I'll tell them she's bleeding," Hoyt said. Janna saw him walk out the door.

"He CAN'T go out there again!" she cried out, trying to rise.

"He won't stay," David said, gently, as he pushed her back down. He put pillows under her legs to elevate them and tucked a warm blanket over her. He pulled off her wet boots and found some warm socks to put on her feet after he'd dried them off.

"He wants to be with Joan," he said as he helped her. "And he's going to tell the paramedics that you're bleeding."

"He's a wonderful man," Janna said.

"He's a wonderful friend," David replied.

The little dogs were pleading to get out. The babies were quiet. The wind howled outside like a banshee. "The dogs-" Janna said, wearily, and closed her eyes. A moment later two furry little creatures with wet noses and teary eyes were bouncing on her and licking her face and hands.

David shooed them off when he came back with the radio. He helped Janna change her pad and the blood soaked jeans. He took a wet cloth and washed her off.

"Do you need some cotton packing to help stop the blood?" he asked.

"We could try it," Janna replied. "I don't think it would hurt to try." David brought back the first aid kit and rolled up some soft cotton. He used it around a tampax and wound gauze around both.

"Maybe the pressure will stop the blood," he said. It was painful and they both cried as David applied the padding. He kept her legs elevated and kept her warm to avoid having her go into shock from loss of blood and the stress she'd been through.

The babies cried and he fixed them a formula. "You need all the fluids you've got," he said, holding a glass of juice to her lips. Janna dozed off to the sound of shrieking winds and things blowing against the house.

David had closed the strong wooden shutters over the windows and it was dark inside the house. A lantern stood on the table throwing off flickers of light.

Janna woke up once and felt to see if there was any new wetness between her legs. She appeared to be dry. She closed her eyes and fell back into an exhausted sleep.

When she awoke Janna realized she was back in the bathtub in the small bathroom. Her breasts hurt and she needed to nurse the babies. The tub had been padded with pillows and her legs had been elevated over the rims with towels under them for padding. She checked again and felt no blood.

She thought of David and how time and again he was there for her. She heard the door open and the clatter of her dogs feet on the floor.

The sound of the wind seemed even louder as David opened the door and came in. The little dogs reared on their hind feet to peek over the edge of the tub at her.

David leaned over and kissed her. She tried to rise but he said, "No, stay still. I think the bleeding has stopped, but we can't take any chances. I don't believe the paramedics will be able to get out here."

"I love you, David," she said.

"Forever," he whispered and kissed her. The babies started to cry and the little dogs whined.

"Okay. We'll feed them!" David laughed. He lifted the babies to Janna's swollen breasts. She relaxed as their tiny mouths began to move with more aggressiveness than the tiny helpless little things seemed to be capable of.

"You're getting to be strong!" she told them. David watched the contented look on

Janna's face as she nursed the babies. He sat watching them until all three were asleep. Then he took the babies and lay them in their makeshift bed.

Janna dozed. She'd been exhausted. She was aware that David and the dogs were in and out of the room at times.

The wind seemed louder when the door was opened. At times she heard the radio. Everything had an unreal quality about it.

At one point David came to sit on the rim of the tub. He asked her a strange question. She thought she might still be asleep. He seemed to be asking if she would be afraid of the grave again.

"Of course not, silly," she'd said, or thought she'd said. "They are a part of us and our babies."

She and David had never filled the graves. They had instead cleared a small trail up to the graves and at times they walked up to leave off a small bouquet of flowers. They'd stand at the gaping hole and say words of love to those below, then they'd drop their floral offering of wild flowers or colorful grasses to the couple who had once lain below. The graves had merged and were one. Vines grew over the cavern below.

Janna slept and woke. David brought the babies to her breast again. He changed their diapers and asked her to check to see if she'd stopped bleeding more than was normal. "I'm still dry," she said, "but I've got to get up and use the toilet."

David had seen to having her sip water occasionally. They had taken a water service and still had several of the large jugs. The island water had never tasted good to Janna.

David said, "I still have that lid around if you could use the 'bed pan.'"

"No," Janna protested. "Please help me get out of here."

The toilet wouldn't flush and David brought in milk jugs of water to flush it.

"Where did these come from?" Janna asked.

"I save the jugs for Hoyt to use on his trot line and have a bunch of them in the big truck," David said. "Fortunately I didn't wait around to fill up every container I could find, for the water is off. I've also gathered up all of our candles, matches, the flashlights and there is oil for the lantern. The kerosene heater is filled with kerosene and I've got extra batteries. I've even filled bottles for the babies in case you somehow can't feed them."

Janna interrupted, "Whyever couldn't I nurse them?"

"I don't know, Janna," David answered, "it just seemed somehow to be the thing to do."

Janna peeked out the bathroom door. The wind seemed to be shaking the house. She saw several bundles outside the door.

"What are those?" she asked.

"Things we might need," David said.

"Then why are they all tied up?" Janna asked. "Do you think the helicopter will be back?"

"No, honey, not until the hurricane is over," David said. He broke off to listen to the radio. The voice sounded frantic. The wind howled and Janna clutched David's arm in fear.

"Please tell me straight," she pleaded.

"We need a storm shelter below ground to be certain that we will be safe," he replied holding her close. "I had no time to dig us one—no time to build. Next year I had thought and had put it off. Janna, this hurricane is one of the worst this coast has ever seen and it's headed straight for the island. The head winds have increased to gale force and much worse. I've fixed us a cave in the graves. Will you do it? Will you trust me? We can't delay—if we wait any longer we'll have to ride it out in the house. I have a strong feeling we'll have to go. Do you think you could make it up the hill? I've tied a rope up the trail to use to pull yourself up and to keep you from being blown over. Could you stay here while I take the babies there first? I've fixed a safe warm nook for them."

Voices called out from the static. David looked frantic. Janna grabbed the clothes David thrust at her.

"Go!" she said "I trust you!"

David lifted up their backpack already lined with blankets. He put their sleeping babies inside and strapped it on facing his chest. He picked up another small bag and rushed out the back door. The wind slammed the door backward with a crash.

Janna saw him stumble, then catch a rope pulled tight between trees along the path to the top of the hill. She clutched her hands to her heart as she watched him fight his way to the top of the hill. The wind blew debris all around. She saw him bend over and disappear.

It seemed an eternity before she saw him returning, without their precious babies. Janna felt a suffocating fear. Their babies were buried—she had to get to them. They were buried with their namesakes—the other Janis and David of long ago.

David burst through the door. He grabbed Janna and the last bag. The little dogs whined. Janna looked at David. "Okay," he yelled, "zip up your jacket and put Muffy down the front. I'll get Puffy!" Muffy snuggled gratefully against Janna—her little wet nose poked out from under Janna's chin and her wet little tongue licked Janna reassuringly.

David put Janna's hand on the rope. "Keep your head down!" he yelled, "and pull yourself up the hill!"

Janna felt David push his body up close behind her. Muffy, thank goodness, kept still. Janna felt things both soft and hard flying into her body as the wind hurtled it along. The thought of her babies drove her up.

The wind was fierce and tried to tear the rope from her hands. The pressure of David's body behind hers pushed her onward. It was sheer hell to hang on to the rope and keep on her feet.

The climb seemed to go on forever. Once she raised her head to see how much further they had to go, and she saw them.

They stood side by side. The wind had no affect on them. They beckoned her on.

She gained new strength. She held tight and fought to keep her feet on the treacherous path. She made it to the graves.

David lifted her into a nest-like cave under the vines. Their babies lay sleeping in a bundle of blankets.

She looked up to thank them but they were gone. She felt peaceful and knew they were all safe.

David worked himself into the mouth of the cave he'd made under the vines. David settled in beside her, putting his arm around her and drawing her to rest against his shoulder.

"They were here with the babies," she said looking up at him.

"Did you see them?" David asked.

"Yes, they beckoned to me when I thought I couldn't keep on," Janna said. She looked around asking, "How did you do this?"

"It wasn't easy," David replied, "and I'm past the meaning of exhaustion. It was you who gave me the strength—you and our babies," David said.

"What did you do to make this so cosy?" she asked.

"First I rolled up my big canvas tarp. Thank God it was in the shed or the wind would have taken it from me like a sail in the wind. I tied it with the long rope and got it up this hill. I lined the hole with the tarp after I'd shoved it down underneath the vines. I tied it to the vines around and over the hole, making a sort of large pouch with it. I made a flap to pull over the opening I left for us to crawl into in case it rains. Then I stamped around making the pocket inside the canvas as large as possible. After that, I took the rope that I had left and tied it to trees on the way down the hill. After that I brought up quilts, pillows, and blankets. Then I brought up supplies and water. I was coming after the last few bags when you had to go to the potty. At that time I heard the radio and found out how close the hurricane actually was to hitting the island, and I knew we'd run out of time."

"And even if it rains a lot we won't get wet down here?" Janna asked, remembering how she had once thought she was in an old well when she'd fallen into the hole.

"Look." David demonstrated how to close off the opening to their snug little cave. "I've even brought you a big pot to pee in!" he said, grinning at her.

"And the puppies?" Janna asked.

"Let's just hope they don't have to go," David answered patting Muffy's head.

One of the babies stirred and Janna patted it's back. It stretched and snuggled back against it's twin. It was growing darker and loud crashes could be heard above.

"I hope the house stands," Janna said, "but even if it doesn't we know we're safe."

"Yes, we are, Honey," David said. "If you get afraid of the dark I have the lantern down here, though I'd rather not light it. I have flashlights to check on the babies and even have extra batteries."

"I'm not afraid," Janna said. She felt very snug and safe even though it sounded like the furies of hell had torn loose above them.

"Do you mind if I just close my eyes and rest awhile?" David asked. He sounded so weary.

"No, Honey, I may do the same," Janna said, though she knew she'd stay awake this time as the sentinel.

David had watched over her for days now—ever since he'd helped to deliver their babies. He had fought for his family long and hard. She wanted him to rest. Soon David slept. His soft breathing joined that of the sleeping puppies. Janna smiled, for Muffy actually snored tiny little snores as she slept.

Baby Janis woke up and she nursed her and just as she fell back to sleep, little David woke up hungry, too. After the babies were back in their soft nest of pillows and blankets, Janna cuddled close to David. He patted her in his sleep. The little dogs snuggled up to Janis's back. "Poor cave people never had it so good as this," Janna thought. "To them this would have been luxury." Janna lay close to her sleeping husband.

Her mind went back to their wedding. She re-lived the day.

**✶✶✶✶✶✶**

A few weeks after Janna and David had read the diary, she realized she was pregnant. She was overwhelmed—this was her first pregnancy.

Janna and David had spoken of marriage. They knew they loved each other, but neither of them felt the need to go thought the actual ceremony. Each day for them was like a beautiful miracle as they now believed it really was.

Janna was writing better than she'd ever written. She was relaxed and happy as she had only dreamed of being. When she found out she was pregnant she was overjoyed. She waited a few more weeks before telling David.

The night she told him had been a night of extraordinary beauty. The stars overhead were thick as a canopy of twinkling lights. The moon was approaching fullness.

Janna had prepared David's favorite meal of grilled grouper, a baked potato, and a nice crisp vegetable salad. For dessert she'd fixed a bowl of fresh berries and sweet cream.

After dinner Janna had asked David to walk on the beach with her. The sand looked like it was paved in silver in the moonlight and millions of stars reflected in the water. The soft rolling waves broke the reflections into constant movement.

Janna had handed David a light blanket to carry along with them. He'd raised his eyebrows at her. "NO," she laughed, "I just thought we could sit and talk. I want to tell you about the first time I ever saw you."

"I KNOW, it was when I came to your house to get the washer and dryer plumbed in."

"No," Janna laughed.

"Was it at the 'Watering Hold" then?" he asked.

Janna laughed again. "Wait until we're on the beach, then I'll tell you!"

They spread the blanket. The sand was still warm. It was heavenly there with the soft sound of the gentle waves and the stars making diamonds in the water.

David leaned over and kissed her. She pulled him close and held him for awhile. Her secret couldn't wait much longer, but first she wanted to tell him about the night she'd seen him rise naked from the water.

She smiled as she remembered how David had laughed, "So! You little voyeur! You were watching me naked!" He kissed her. "You're shameless!" he continued teasing.

"You were like a God rising from the sea. It was so beautiful. I think it was then that I knew you. I think it was the moment of our reunion; you know, from the past."

"Remember the other one?" David said. "That's how she first saw HER David."

"I wanted to tell you when we read the diary, but it was so confusing—I needed to absorb it—it was so unbelievable and yet it was real. I felt like two people. I still do, often,—both she and me. She is me and I am her."

"I know," David said.

"Now there's more," Janna said. She took David's face between her hands. She looked into his beautiful eyes. "Honey, we're going to have a baby."

David was motionless for a moment. His eyes widened and he suddenly took her in his arms. He pulled her onto his lap and held her close.

"I didn't think I could father a child," he said.

"I didn't think I could become pregnant," Janna said. "Should you be out here like this?" David asked. "You won't get chilled or anything will you?"

Janna shoved him playfully. "No, silly!" she giggled, "It's warm out anyway! I think we've both got a lot to learn!"

She thought of the books they'd bought and the ones they'd checked out from the library on the mainland. Then one day they found out they were having twins.

They had chosen two names only—Janis and David. "They will be united through our babies," Janna said. "They will be as one." They had no doubt that the twins would be a boy and a girl. It was destiny. They knew it in their hearts.

They began to plan the wedding.

Janna wiggled closer to David as she thought of the wedding. Muffy and Puffy pressed closer to her back. The babies and David slept peacefully. The winds above ground shrieked and crashed all around them. Janna lay against David feeling strangely safe and happy.

The day of the wedding couldn't have been more beautiful. None of Janna's family had been able to come. Janie's twins were still so tiny. She was nursing them and then there were the other children. Jake was busy with the farm and couldn't get away—everyone wanted them to come there. Janna wanted the wedding to be on the beach at the island. She knew it had to he that way. There had been many phone calls and presents poured in from Iowa for the two of them.

Janie and Jake gave Janna the most wonderful gift. Janna was stunned when she got the deed for the island property.

Janie and Jake had put aside a share of the farm Janie and Janna had inherited from their parents. They had started the account for Janna years ago. Janna had refused to touch the money for she'd never put any work into the farm.

Janie had equated the money fairly. She'd explained this to Janna more than once. She'd allowed for the lack of participation and expenditure. She'd been fair and wouldn't accept any portion she'd considered to be Janna's.

Janna had never thought of the money even though she had fluctuated drastically at times financially. "It's either the feast or the famine for me!" she'd laugh as she waited to see if something she'd written had sold or if she'd just overspent her resources in a fit of generosity. The checks always beat the wolf when he hovered at her door, for she worked well under pressure. Often her best writing came as a result of pressure.

Janna was a survivor. She had always known she was a survivor. Many farmers might have the will to survive that Janna did, but with them there were often that unforeseen season of drought, the weather, pests, the government, etc. that could take unexpected tolls. Janna had let the money ride, considering it only as a slush fund should the farm run into problems. Jake's good sense had kept that from happening.

Both Janna and Janie had access to the money. Janna had never planned to use the money for herself—Janie knew that. Just as Janie had persuaded the relatives to buy the property so far away as time-shares, she persuaded them to sell it back to her as a gift for Janna. She told them they could still take vacations there—as guests of Janna and David. They agreed.

Janna had stood with the deed in her hand—tears ran down her face. After so many years of running here and there she had finally come home.

Janie had also enclosed another gift. The gift told her beyond any shadow of a doubt that she'd found what she'd been searching for all of her life.

Janie had researched family history. Centuries before there had been a Nora Nashiem. She had married a Jonathan Diehl from Boston. Her husband had died in a hurricane that had destroyed one of his ships.

Nora and her two daughters had been visiting relatives in Iowa at that time.

The younger daughter, Janna, had married a prosperous Iowa farmer.

The eldest daughter, strangely named Jana also, but with one 'n', had never married. The elder girl became a school teacher of some renown. A number of years separated the ages of the girls and the younger one was called little Jan.

"Our family can't seem to get past those 'J' names," Janie had written.

Janna and David were certain that baby David had also survived to become David's ancestor. The diary had made it clear.

With these priceless gifts and a beautiful wedding day, their marriage had been perfect.

They were married in the house. Janna thought of the dress she had worn. It was old fashioned of a style worn in the seventeen hundreds. A crown of wild flowers held the antique lace veil on top of her braided hair. It fell to the tips of her fingers. The ivory lace was fragile and Janna looked as thought she had stepped from the past.

David's old fashioned waistcoat and cravat were also period pieces. They found a tall beaver hat that they had used for some special wedding photos.

The wedding ceremony was performed with Janna and David standing halfway up the stairs. The minister stood a few steps above them. One single bouquet adorned the banister beside them. It decorated the space just above the carving that proclaimed "Janis and David forever", carved there so many years before. Only they knew the significance of the bouquet.

They had written their own vows. They did not include the words 'until death do us part' for they knew that death would never be a barrier to their love. Instead they vowed to be joined for eternity. After David had kissed her there on the stair they both touched the place below the bouquet.

The wedding had been an open invitation for all of the islanders. It had been informal with the exception of the bridal couple. Janna had turned on the stairway and thrown the bouquet she held. Joan had caught it. After the bouquet was thrown, Janna and David fled hand in hand—they ran together out the front door to freedom. They knew who they ran for. They were wed and their babies went with them safe in Janna's body.

It had taken centuries for it to happen.

Everyone ran behind them as they flew to the beach. Long tables had been set up there. The

231

wedding cake had been fashioned like a sand castle. A tiny king and queen stood on the parapets. There were tubs of oysters on ice. Hoyt had supplied the oysters. Fish was smoking on huge grills. A whole hog was waiting to be lifted from the smoker garnished with big red apples. There were salads, breads, John Henry's famous chicken and dumplings and enough food for an army. The owners of the 'Watering Hole' had prepared the buffet.

After the cake was cut and the toasts were drunk (Janna drank gingerale) she and David had slipped back to the house to change into cutoffs and tee shirts.

They held each other close after changing clothes. A sound like soft singing wafted through the house—it had the sound of a nursery song—the words were soft and blurred. David had placed his hand on Janna's stomach and the babies moved for the first time at that moment.

"Was that the babies?" David asked in wonder.

"Yes, I think so," Janna replied.

"What did it feel like?" he'd asked.

"Sort of like butterflies—that's the best description I can think of," she told him. They held each other close for awhile longer and then joined their wedding party.

******

Janna lay smiling. Peace and precious memories filled her heart as the hurricane raged above. She kissed David's back. He stirred and made a little sound. Janna snuggled down and in spite of her intent to be vigilant, she fell asleep.

Janna awoke to Puffy scratching her shoulder
with her paw. The sky above the little cave
was light and she realized that there was no
longer a howling wind and crashing sounds
above. The wind seemed to moan softly instead.
Puffy pawed her again and she heard a tiny
cry.

"My babies!" she thought frantically. She
sat up and reached for little Janis and baby
David. They both began to cry. "They're
hungry!" she thought and wondered if they'd
been crying long before Puffy woke her up. The
babies were wet but she fed them first.

David sat up as she reached for the babies.
"Did I sleep all night?" he asked.

"We all did!" Janna said. The babies nursed
for awhile, then David reached for little
David. Puffy whined and wriggled around. Muffy
had her nose pointed at the opening in the
cave and was sniffing.

"I think the hurricane is over and these
little critters want out." He placed little
David back next to Janis as he scooted past
them. Janna moved over and placed her back to
their pillows and held both babies to her
swollen breasts.

"Whew! Someone needs changing," she laughed.
David stood in the close confines of their
shelter and lifted the dogs out one by one.

"I'll scout around while you finish feeding
the babies if you're not afraid here alone for
a few minutes," he said.

"Don't be long. I need to stretch and I'm
bursting to pee," Janna said.

"Want out now?" David asked.

"Maybe I'd better," she said. David pulled
himself out of the narrow opening then reached
down.

"Can you pull out one of the sleeping bags?" he asked. Janna laid the babies back on their blankets. They both cried out. They weren't through nursing.

"Wait a second, little piggies," she told them as she poked the sleeping bag up for David.

"Now hand the babies up," he said, reaching downward, "then their diaper bag. I'll get the rest later."

Janna reached the crying babies up to David then he reached down for her. She stepped behind a pile of fallen branches to relieve herself. She removed the packing and only a little blood tinged the tissue she'd taken with her.

Janna thanked God for the survival of her family. From the top of the hill, she could see that the house still stood though there was evidence of damage. Trees were down, many of them twisted off their roots and piles of debris lay against obstacles that had caught it in passing.

Waves on the bayshore were turbulent. A warm tropical wind blew steadily with a soft howling sound. The hurricane had passed.

Janna sat down to finish nursing the babies while David took the rest of their things from the graves. He had spread the sleeping bag out for them. Muffy and Puffy were dashing around the hillside sniffing and yapping at squirrels and birds.

The babies' tiny mouths moved against her breasts and she was grateful and happy.

David took their things down the hillside then came up for Janna and the babies. The trail was filled with limbs of trees, boards, pieces of tin and other things. The rope was still there but not as snugly tied, for a couple of the trees it had been wound around had been sheared of their roots.

The back porch had glass missing all around. Leaves and twigs lay everywhere. Books lay scattered around where they'd been ripped from the bookcases and slammed into the walls. The kitchen and living room was a mess, but still wasn't a total wreck. The tiny bath where they'd hidden and where the babies had been born had a tree trunk driven through it's door. It had come through the front window taking part of the house with it.

Janna and David lay the sleeping babies on a pallet and went upstairs very carefully.

Halfway up the stairs Janna paused and whispered, "Thank you."

"Me, too," David said.

The hallway upstairs was piled with their bedding. They threaded their way through soggy mattresses, wet bedding and clothing. A beautiful tiffany lamp had smashed to pieces against a wall. The wardrobe from what had been one of the guest rooms lay splintered with its contents spilled out in tattered ruins.

They made their way down the hallway to their bedroom. They forced open the door. The window had been blown out.

Heavy shutters had been closed over all the windows with the exception of the garden room. David had nailed plywood over the windows there.

Massive iron bolts had held the heavy wooden shutters together. Most of the shutters had held. One had been torn loose downstairs when the tree had been driven into it, crossing the room and slamming through the bathroom door.

David and Janna stood in the doorway of their room. It had been attacked with a fury.

The big bed was strewn with debris from outside and the other furniture has been tossed about the room as though hurled from the hands of a giant. Janna glanced to the gaping window and saw that the seat below the window was still intact.

The mattress on the big brass bed had been laid open. Janna gasped when she saw the large shard of glass stabbed through the mattress where she usually lay. A huge piece of driftwood had smashed through the window and lay at the foot of the mattress. The force of the old board had probably driven the shard of glass before it to stab into the bed.

David turned the old piece of driftwood over. It was a piece from a thick old plank. He said, "Honey, look at this." His voice was strange.

`Janna looked up from the pewter candlestick she had pulled from under some of the clothing. David read aloud from the deeply carved words still legible on the plank.

"LADY NORA."

Janna leaned against David. Her legs were weak as she looked from the piece of the old ship to the dagger of glass shoved deep into her bed.

"It's from his ship, David. After all these centuries, he surfaced and joined the hurricane for his revenge. Do you remember it was glass that pierced the body of Janis when she tried to escape? He MUST have been insane. The sunken ship must have been drug up by the violence of the wind and water, the same sort of untamed violence he must have felt himself."

Muffy barked loudly and Janna yelled out, "Oh God! The babies!"

They rushed down the stairs to find the babies sound asleep and Muffy facing off a little lost kitten.

"Shame on you, Muffy!" Janna scolded and Muffy looked up at her. "Naughty, naughty!" Janna said and Muffy went over to lick the bedraggled little kitten. The kitten rubbed itself against Muffy and that was all it took to win her over. "You softy!" Janna teased Muffy as she leaned over to pet her and the kitten.

"We can't stay here until we fix the house back up," David said. "It will take a while to clean this all up and restore it." He held Janna close. "We've been very fortunate," he said.

Janna snuggled against his chest.

"If we gather up a few things we can walk slowly and go to the 'Watering Hole.' Someone can probably get us to the mainland, or we can find somewhere to stay. Or would you like to take the babies and stay with Janie and Jake in Iowa until I get this house back together?" David asked.

"No," Janna said, thinking of another Jana who had gone to Iowa never to return to the island. "We're staying together," she said.

They took their time as they took the beach side of the route to the little village. They worked their way over heaps of blackish green seaweed, torn from its beds far below the water's surface, to be flung upon the beach and left stranded there in soggy heaps. Driftwood, branches, old weathered boards and logs littered the beautiful beach.

David carried the babies and Janna carried a backpack and diaper~bag, stuffed full of baby things.

The devastation was far worse than they could have imagined. It was amazing that their home had weathered the hurricane as well as it had. Most of the beautiful homes that had dotted the area along the beach toward the village had been destroyed. Their wreckage was everywhere.

As they approached the place where the 'Watering Hole' had been they saw only scattered piles of rubble. People were gathered around in groups talking. The big new fire truck lay on its side. The center of the tiny community had been destroyed.

David stood a picnic table upright and someone helped him drag it out from the pile of trash it had been sticking out of. David spread out the sleeping bag he'd tied to his back and she lay the babies down on it, and climbed up to sit beside them. David put their bags down beside her and walked over to talk to some of the people standing in a group.

Janna searched through the side pocket of the larger bag and found her wallet with some cash and her checkbook. She had packed some important papers in the bag, also. The deed to the house and her marriage license were with them. She looked up to see David walking toward her. She started to smile until she saw his face. She held out her arms and he came into them. "What's wrong, Honey?" she asked.

"Hoyt and Joan were in the 'Watering Hole' when it collapsed," he said, tears ran down his face.

"Are they-?" Janna couldn't complete the sentence.

"They were found in each other's arms. They apparently went together."

Janna held David close. "I'm so sorry," she whispered.

"I lost some other friends as well," David said, "but he was like a brother." Janna held him for long moments before he spoke.

"Janna, a boat is coming to take people off the island. Shelters have been set up and I'm sending you and the babies over. I'll join you tonight at some point. Jay will see you safely over. He has to take his little girl over, too. He'll let me know where you are. You'll be safe.

"We have a lot of work to do here. A number of people are dead, many were injured and some are still missing. I'm needed here."

"I understand," Janna said. "It's okay—just take care of yourself for us."

"We're protected," David said.

Janna looked into his eyes. "Yes, I know," she answered.

On the boat to the mainland, Jay told Janna of the rumors that a number of people had said they'd seen a large old-fashioned ship riding the violent waves in the midst of the hurricane.

He said timbers of an old ship had been found scattered about the shore of the bay. The wreckage had obviously been that of an old ship long since sunk and dredged up by the violent tides the hurricane had produced.

Janna shuddered. She knew who's ship it had been.

# ABOUT THE AUTHOR

Janis was born and raised in Arkansas.

She attended several colleges in the U.S.A., Spain and Germany.

She doesn't remember a time when she didn't love to write. She's published several newspaper articles, some poetry and done a piece on TV for an organization for battered women.

She has worked with the elderly for the last twenty years and wrote in the precious moments she could seize to move toward her dream of being a novelist. She is currently working on another book.